From Sacred Song to Ritual Music

Twentieth-Century Understandings of Roman Catholic Worship Music

Jan Michael Joncas

A Liturgical Press Book

THE LITURGICAL PRESS
Collegeville, Minnesota

2	3	4	5	6	7	8

Library of Congress Cataloging in Publication Data

Joncas, Jan Michael.
    From sacred song to ritual music : twentieth-century
understandings of Roman Catholic worship music / Jan Michael Joncas.
        p. cm.
    Includes bibliographical references and index.
    ISBN (invalid) 0-8146-2352-2
    1. Church music—Catholic Church—20th century. 2. Catholic
Church—Liturgy—History—20th century.   I. Title.
ML3007.J66   1997
264'.0202—dc20
                                                                96-43857
                                                                    CIP
                                                                    MN

CONTENTS

Preface

Annie Dillard, Pulitzer Prize-winning author of *Pilgrim at Tinker's Creek* and *Holy the Firm*, sketches the following scene familiar to late twentieth-century Roman Catholics in her collection of essays *Teaching a Stone to Talk:*

> There is a singing group in the Catholic church today, a singing group which calls itself "Wildflowers." The lead is a tall, square-jawed teen-aged boy, buoyant and glad to be here. He carries a guitar; he plucks out a little bluesy riff and hits some chords. With him are the rest of the Wildflowers. There is an old woman, wonderfully determined; she has long orange hair and is dressed country-and-western style. A long embroidered strap around her neck slings a big western guitar low over her pelvis. Beside her stands a frail, withdrawn fourteen-year-old boy, and a large Chinese man in his twenties who seems to want to enjoy himself but is not quite sure how to. He looks around wildly as he sings, and shuffles his feet. There is also a very tall teen-aged girl; she is delicate of feature, half serene and half petrified, a wispy soprano. They straggle out in front of the altar and teach us a brand-new hymn.
>
> It all seems a pity at first, for I have overcome a fiercely anti-Catholic upbringing in order to attend Mass simply and solely to escape Protestant guitars. Why am I here? Who gave these nice Catholics guitars? Why are they not mumbling in Latin and performing superstitious rituals? What is the Pope thinking of?[1]

Who gave these nice Catholics guitars? . . . What is the Pope thinking of? These plangent sentences raise in a humorous way the topic that this short study attempts to address. What are the shifts in understanding, signaled in various papal, conciliar, curial, bishops' conference, and collaborative scholarly documents, that have led to such changes in Roman Catholic worship music practice during the twentieth century?

To that end I will first list, describe, and situate the nine documents chosen for examination. The bulk of the study will note how these documents respond to five questions: (1) What is Roman Catholic worship music? (2) What is the purpose of Roman Catholic worship music?

(3) What qualities should Roman Catholic worship music exhibit? (4) What people are to make Roman Catholic worship music? (5) What instruments are to make Roman Catholic worship music? A short conclusion will highlight some topics that call for further reflection.

The limits of this study should be made clear. First of all, I am deliberately limiting my reflections to Roman Catholic worship music. While much wonderful worship music and thoughtful evaluation has been produced in other Christian denominations, I judge that I can write most authentically about my own religious heritage. Second, my reflections are confined to Roman Rite worship music. One of the glories of Roman Catholicism is its unity in diversity manifested in multiple rites, both Eastern (e.g., Coptic, Ethiopic, Armenian, Chaldean, Byzantine) and Western (e.g., Ambrosian, Mozarabic, Celtic, Gallican). Just as each of these rites has produced its own characteristic liturgical forms and spirituality observable in texts, postures, gestures, vesture, architecture, and artifacts, so each of these rites has produced a distinctive body of worship music. Nevertheless I confine my analysis to the worship music of the Roman Rite, both for reasons of length and of competence. Third, I limit my documentation of changing attitudes about Roman Catholic worship music to papal, conciliar, and curial documents for the Roman Rite throughout the world, and then narrow my focus to bishops' conference and scholarly documents produced in the United States. While many excellent insights about Roman Catholic worship music have appeared in other languages (especially German, French, Italian, and Spanish) and other cultures of the English-speaking world (especially Canadian, English, Irish, and Australian), I feel most competent to reflect on the theories and practices marking the United States' liturgical renewal.

I thank Dr. Kim Kasling who invited me to address the Seventeenth Annual Liturgical Music Workshop at St. John's University (Collegeville, Minnesota) 13–15 June 1994 on the topic "Liturgical Music: Defining Quality, Defining Choice." This study reprises much of the material I presented at that workshop with further insights gained from interaction with the participants. Thanks are also due to Fr. Michael Naughton, O.S.B., who graciously accepted the manuscript and guided it through the process of preparation for publication.

I dedicate this study to Vicki Klima, director of the Office of Worship of the Archdiocese of St. Paul and Minneapolis, Minnesota. Vicki and I have had a long and enriching friendship, sharing academic studies, pastoral work at Presentation of the Blessed Virgin Mary Catholic Church in Maplewood, Minnesota (where I served as associate pastor and she as liturgy director in the early 1980s), the production of musical compositions (where I have set her lyrics and she has offered inclusive language corrections of some of my earlier compositions), and recording (where she has graced my albums as both soloist and chorus member). More important than these, however, has been her witness as a woman of faith to the importance of the Church's worship, to the need for scholarship and pastoral practice to remain in dialogue, and to commitment to a life of justice and charity as a necessary consequence of engaging liturgical worship.

    Soli Deo gloria!

Fr. Jan Michael Joncas
University of St. Thomas
St. Paul, Minnesota
June 1996

ENDNOTE

[1] Annie Dillard, *Teaching a Stone to Talk: Expeditions and Encounters* (New York: Harper and Row, 1982) 18–19.

Abbreviations

BCL   Bishops' Committee on the Liturgy of the National Conference of Catholic Bishops (USA)

DOL   International Commission on English in the Liturgy, *Documents on the Liturgy 1963–1979: Conciliar, Papal, and Curial Texts* (Collegeville: The Liturgical Press, 1982).

GIRM   General Instruction of the Roman Missal

LMT   Liturgical Music Today

MCW   Music in Catholic Worship

MR   The Milwaukee Symposia for Church Composers: A Ten-Year Report

MS   Musicam Sacram

MSD   Musicae sacrae disciplina

SC   Sacrosanctum Concilium

SS   The Snowbird Statement on Catholic Liturgical Music

TLD   *The Liturgy Documents: A Parish Resource,* 3d ed. (Chicago: Liturgy Training Publications, 1991).

TLS   Tra le sollecitudini

1958Inst   De musica sacra et sacra liturgia ad mentem litterarum Pii Papae XII "Musicae sacrae disciplina" et "Mediator Dei"

Introduction:
Situating the Documents

The nine documents examined in this study were created at different times in the twentieth century by different Roman Catholic ecclesiastical institutions, are addressed to different audiences, and represent different levels of teaching authority. Before analyzing how each of these documents treats Roman Rite worship music, an attempt should be made to situate each document in its historical context, to clarify the range of the document's intended auditors, and to identify the quality and extent of its authority.

Tra le sollecitudini[1]

A papal instruction having the "force of law as a canonical code concerning sacred music," *Tra le sollecitudini* [hereafter TLS] grounds the project of liturgical music reform for the Roman Rite in the twentieth century. Issued *motu proprio et ex certa scientia* by Pius X on 22 November 1903 (the feast of Saint Cecilia, patroness of music), it brought to a climax a series of reform decrees that the pope had issued in his earlier offices as bishop of Mantua and cardinal-patriarch of Venice. Substantially the work of Fr. Angelo De Santi, S.J., but with Pius X's personal corrections, TLS articulated general principles for sacred music, differentiated its various kinds, treated liturgical texts, gave guidelines for the external form of sacred compositions, presented legislation concerning singers and instrumentalists at worship and the length of liturgical chant, and suggested various means for developing proper sacred music.

The broad scope of the document's intended audience is obvious from its concluding article:

> 29. . . . We desire all choirmasters, singers, and clerics, all superiors of
> seminaries, ecclesiastical institutions, and religious communities, all

parish priests and rectors of churches, all canons of collegiate and cathe-dral churches, and, most especially, the Ordinaries of all Dioceses, zeal-ously to support these wise reforms, which have been long desired and unanimously hoped for by all, in order that no injury be done to the au-thority of the Church, which has often proposed them and now insists on them once more.

Though not expressly stated in TLS, it is clear that the liturgical legis-lation contained therein only applies to the music of the Roman Rite, although the principles concerning sacred music might find wider ap-plication in other Eastern and Western rites.

John Huels clarifies the authoritative "weight" of an apostolic let-ter issued *motu proprio:*

> When the pope wishes to create new law . . . he promulgates it princi-pally by means of the documents known as the "apostolic constitution" or the "apostolic letter motu proprio.". . . The apostolic letter motu pro-prio is so-called because the pope acts on his own initiative in creating new legislation in his own name rather than merely approving a decree or other document issued in the name of a curial congregation.[2]

Thus TLS should be considered foundational liturgical legislation con-cerning music for the Roman Rite until modified by Pius XII's author-ity and superseded by the reforms stemming from the Vatican Council II. The importance of TLS can be seen in how frequently it is quoted in later papal, conciliar, curial, and territorial bishops' conference texts.

Musicae sacrae disciplina[3]

Although other twentieth-century popes followed Pius X's lead in treating sacred music,[4] the next great papal document on Roman Rite worship music was issued by Pius XII on 25 December 1955. Entitled *Musicae sacrae disciplina* [hereafter MSD], this lengthy encyclical letter provides a historical conspectus of the development of Roman Catholic worship music, presents some philosophical reflections on the relation of art and worship, expands on TLS's list of the qualities sacred music must exhibit, relaxes some of the prohibitions given in TLS, and coun-sels various approaches to improving the quality and performance of sacred music.

As an encyclical letter, MSD is addressed to the Catholic bishops of the world, addressed as "venerable brethren" throughout the docu-ment. Although it is a papal product, MSD does not bear the same weight as TLS; as Kevin Seasoltz remarks:

Encyclicals are divided into two categories: encyclical epistles and encyclical letters. Those of the first category are more solemn in form, although the content may not always be more important than that of other papal letters. Encyclicals are generally pastoral letters written by the pope for the universal Church. Rather than affirming dogmatic definitions, they usually attempt to clarify doctrinal issues. They express the pope's ordinary teaching authority; their content, then, is capable of development and change. Encyclicals are not legislative in the sense that they modify existing laws of the Church.[5]

Thus MSD is to be interpreted as a commentary on TLS, expanding upon its prescriptions rather than modifying or abrogating them.

De musica sacra et sacra liturgia ad mentem litterarum Pii Papae XII "Musicae sacrae disciplina" et "Mediator Dei"[6]

One of the final documents to appear during the pontificate of Pius XII, an *Instruction on Music and Liturgy* [hereafter 1958Inst] was promulgated by a Roman curial agency, the Sacred Congregation of Rites, on 3 September 1958 (then the feast of Saint Pius X). This lengthy document begins with explanations of the terminology employed and statements of the general norms on the use of sacred music in the liturgy. The bulk of the document is taken up with particular norms: the use of music in various situations (Mass, Divine Office, benediction), the different kinds of worship music, the books of liturgical chant, the use of instruments, the people who make worship music, and programs to cultivate worship music and liturgy.

Seasoltz sketches how curial documents are to be weighted, with specific remarks about curial instructions:

> Among the most important documents issued by the Roman Congregations, Secretariats, and Offices are decrees, instructions, declarations, circular letters, directories, official responses, and norms. . . . An *instruction* is a doctrinal explanation or a set of directives, recommendations, or admonitions issued by the Roman curia. It usually elaborates on prescriptions so that they may be more effectively implemented. Strictly speaking, an instruction does not have the force of universal law or definition. If by chance an instruction cannot be reconciled with a given law, the law itself is to be preferred over the instruction.[7]

Thus 1958Inst presents itself as an extension of TLS and MSD, applying the principles and directives found in those documents to particular situations faced by the worshiping communities of the Roman Catholic world.

Sacrosanctum Concilium[8]

On 4 December 1963, Pope Paul VI, in union with the Fathers of the Second Vatican Council, promulgated *Sacrosanctum Concilium* [hereafter SC], the Constitution on the Sacred Liturgy. The first of the conciliar documents to be issued, SC transformed the way Roman Catholics had worshiped since the time of the liturgical reforms after the Council of Trent.

After an introduction that sketches the goals of the Vatican Council II in general, the first chapter of SC provides general principles for the restoration and promotion of the liturgy. This chapter is of foundational importance and includes: (1) a disquisition on the nature of the Church's liturgy and its importance in ecclesial life (arts. 5–13); (2) an exhortation on promoting liturgical instruction and active participation of the faithful (arts. 14–20); (3) norms for the reform of the liturgy: general (arts. 22–25), those drawn from its hierarchic and communal nature (articles 26–32), those based upon its didactic and pastoral nature (arts. 33–36), and those intended to adapt liturgy to the culture and tradition of various peoples (arts. 37–40); (4) guidelines for promoting liturgical life in dioceses and parishes (arts. 41–42); and (5) suggestions for promoting "pastoral-liturgical action" (arts. 43–46). Subsequent chapters combine theoretical reflections, usually in the first few articles of the chapter, with practical decrees of various degrees of universality. Chapter two treats the Eucharist (arts. 47–58), chapter three the other sacraments and sacramentals, including the consecration of virgins, rites of religious profession, and Christian funerals (arts. 59–82). The Divine Office is treated in chapter four (arts. 83–101) and the Liturgical Year in chapter five (arts. 102–11). Chapter six (arts. 112–21) deals with sacred music, while sacred art is the concern of chapter seven (arts. 122–30).

Seasoltz clarifies the intended audience and authoritative status of this document:

> Since an ecumenical council represents the whole Church and has full power over it, documents originating in that context are of supreme importance in the Church. Four types of documents were issued by the Second Vatican Council: constitutions, decrees, declarations, and messages. . . . Distinctions among the various categories are not always easily and clearly drawn, but in general, *constitutions* are addressed to the universal Church and are concerned with doctrinal, disciplinary, or pastoral issues of the greatest importance. Four constitutions were issued by the Second Vatican Council: on the liturgy, the Church, divine revelation, and the Church in the modern world.[9]

But Frederick McManus nuances Seasoltz's assessment by noting the peculiar character of this constitution:

> It is by no means a dogmatic constitution (like *Lumen Gentium* and *Dei Verbum* of Vatican II) or a pastoral constitution (the compromise terminology adopted for *Gaudium et spes*, which is neither a dogmatic nor a disciplinary document). Formally the liturgical constitution is a disciplinary conciliar decree (with the added dignity and significance of a more solemn "constitution"), as is evident from its recurring juridical language: ". . . Therefore the holy council decrees the following. . . ."[10]

Thus SC, while containing a mixture of theological reflection, legislative prescription, and pastoral exhortation, has authoritative status comparable to TLS for post-Vatican II Roman Catholics. Note that article three of SC states that its prescriptions apply directly only to the Roman Rite; its theological vision, however, touches the other rites:

> Among the principles and norms there are some which can and should be applied both to the Roman Rite and also to all other rites. The practical norms which follow, however, should be taken as applying only to the Roman rite, except for those which, in the very nature of things, affect other rites as well.

Musicam Sacram[11]

On 5 March 1967, the Sacred Congregation for Divine Worship, a Roman curial agency, issued an instruction on sacred music entitled *Musicam Sacram* [hereafter MS]. Not "a collection of all the legislation on sacred music, but a statement simply of the principal norms that seem most needed at this time" [MS 3], the document presents itself as a continuation of the 1964 instruction by the Sacred Congregation of Rites (predecessor of the Sacred Congregation for Divine Worship) on the proper implementation of SC. After sketching a definition of sacred music and its purpose in Roman Catholic liturgy, the document lists some general norms; distinguishes the roles of various participants in the liturgy; offers guidelines on singing at Mass, during the Liturgy of the Hours, at various sacraments and sacramentals, in celebrations of the Liturgical Year, and as part of Bible services and popular devotions; presents norms for preserving the treasury of sacred music and the use of traditional and vernacular languages in the Roman Rite; exhorts composers in their work of providing musical settings for vernacular liturgical texts; notes the proper use of instrumental music during worship; and calls for the establishment and support of various institutions to promote sacred music.

As 1958Inst served as an extension of TLS and MSD, so MS applies the principles and directives found in SC to particular situations faced by the worshiping communities of the Roman Catholic world. It has the same weight for post-Vatican II Roman Rite worship as 1958Inst had for pre-Vatican II Roman Rite worship.

Music in Catholic Worship[12]

In contrast to the papal, conciliar, and curial documents intended for the universal Roman Rite considered above, the next two documents are the products of a territorial bishops' conference, technically applicable only to that territory.

In 1972 the Bishops' Committee on the Liturgy of the National Conference of Catholic Bishops (USA) [hereafter BCL] issued *Music in Catholic Worship* [hereafter MCW]; a second edition (slightly revised for inclusive language) appeared in 1983. After an introduction noting how the BCL had issued a document on the place of music in eucharistic celebrations in 1967, MCW begins with a theology of liturgical celebration (arts. 1–9). A second segment deals with pastoral planning for liturgical celebration (arts. 10–14), specifying that attention must be paid to the congregation (arts. 15–18), the occasion (arts. 19–20), and the celebrant (arts. 21–22). The heart of MCW appears in the next section on the place of music in liturgical celebration. After explicating how music serves the expression of faith (arts. 23–24), MCW articulates its now famous threefold judgment in evaluating music in liturgical celebration (art. 25): (1) musical (arts. 26–29); (2) liturgical (art. 30) as manifest in structural requirements (art. 31), textual demands (art. 32), and role differentiation (arts. 33–38); and (3) pastoral (arts. 39–41). MCW then offers general considerations of the liturgical structure of the Eucharist (arts. 44–49) and applies its principles of liturgical celebration to music in eucharistic worship, both generally (arts. 50–52) and specifically in the categories of acclamations (arts. 53–59), processional songs (arts. 60–62), responsorial psalms (art. 63), ordinary chants (arts. 64–69), and supplementary songs (arts. 70–74). Articles 75–78 treat progress and new directions in liturgical music composition and performance. After some cursory remarks on music in sacramental celebrations (arts. 79–83), MCW concludes with a call for further development in Roman Catholic worship music.

What authority does such a document hold? According to canon 1257 of the 1917 Code of Canon Law, only the Apostolic See had the authority to enact liturgical laws. Diocesan bishops were expected to exercise vigilance in making sure that liturgical law was scrupulously observed in their territory; the only laws they could promulgate touching the liturgy were those to enforce the decrees and rules stemming from the Apostolic See. But reflecting SC 22.1, which states that "regulation of the liturgy depends solely on the authority of the Church, that is, on the Apostolic See *and, accordingly as the law determines, on the bishop*" [emphasis added], the 1983 Code of Canon Law recognizes the authority of both the diocesan bishop and territorial bishops' conferences in certain areas of liturgical legislation (see canons 135.2; 391; 392; 455; 678.1; 835.1; 838.3–4; 891; 961.2).

John Huels offers the following clarifications on the legislative weight of documents issued by a territorial bishops' conference:

> Diocesan bishops and conferences of bishops possess real authority over the liturgy and can enact legislation affecting the liturgy. . . . However, often the regulations they issue are not true laws because they are not promulgated as such. They appear as guidelines or pastoral directives. This does not mean that their observance is optional, but it indicates that the authority who issued them does not wish them to have the same "weight" that the law itself possesses.[13]

Thus MCW should be considered a set of pastoral guidelines applying the prescriptions of SC and MS to the situation of the United States. While other territories may find the positions taken in MCW to be helpful, their practice is to be guided by whatever prescriptions their own territorial bishops' conference has issued or, in the absence of such a document, SC and MS.

Liturgical Music Today[14]

Appearing in 1982, *Liturgical Music Today* [hereafter LMT] was also issued by the BCL. Article 3 makes it clear that LMT is intended by its authors as a commentary upon and extension of MCW:

> Since the Roman liturgical books were still in the process of revision ten years ago, the Committee recognizes that there are subjects that *Music in Catholic Worship* addressed only briefly or not at all, such as music within the sacramental rites and in the Liturgy of the Hours. Moreover, the passage of time has raised a number of unforeseen issues in need of clarification and questions revealing new possibilities for liturgical music. We take this opportunity to note these developments. This statement, therefore, should be read as a companion to *Music in Catholic Worship* and *Environment and Art in Catholic Worship*.

After a short introduction (arts. 1–5), LMT reinforces many of the general principles found in MCW: issues concerning the structure of the liturgy (arts. 6–7); the place, function, and form of song in liturgy (arts. 8–11); various pastoral concerns (art. 12); progressive solemnity (art. 13); and language and musical idioms (arts. 14–15). Music in Eucharist is treated in articles 16–21; its role in Christian initiation (arts. 22–26), reconciliation (art. 27), Christian marriage (arts. 28–29), and Christian burial (arts. 30–33) also comes under comment. Articles 34–45 treat music in the Liturgy of the Hours. LMT then addresses a variety of topics: music and the Liturgical Year (arts. 46–48), music of the past (arts. 49–53), music and the cultural heritage (arts. 54–55), instrumental and recorded music at liturgy (arts. 56–62), music ministry (arts. 63–70), and copyright (arts. 71–72). The conclusion (arts. 73–74) reiterates MCW's call for further progress in the development and execution of Roman Catholic worship music.

The final two documents to be analyzed fit none of the categories so far discussed.

The Milwaukee Symposia for Church Composers: A Ten-Year Report[15]

On 9 July 1992 a group of twenty-nine liturgists, text-writers, musicians, composers, and pastoral practitioners issued "A Ten Year Report" on the Milwaukee Symposia for Church Composers [hereafter MR]. Responding to a suggestion from the late Sr. Theophane Hytrek, S.S.S.F., Archbishop Rembert Weakland, O.S.B., hosted five symposia in 1982, 1985, 1988, 1990, and 1992 involving a total of sixty-seven participants. Generated between 1990 and 1992 under the editorial guidance of Edward Foley, Capuchin, MR has no status comparable to papal, conciliar, curial, or territorial bishops' conference texts. Rather as the foreword states:

> It is a report on ten years of observation, study, reflection and dialogue concerning the nature and quality of liturgical music in the United States, especially within the Roman Catholic tradition. . . . We are convinced that this report can be a springboard for broader and deeper discussion of some of the concerns that have brought us together: more collaboration among composers, liturgists and text writers; a better understanding of the role of art in the liturgy; the need to develop a solid repertoire of liturgical music; a fuller understanding of Christian ritual action; and an ongoing commitment to the active participation of every Christian in the liturgy. . . . We know that this report carries only the weight of the knowledge and insights of the participants. We placed more emphasis on the quality of the questions raised than upon the solutions proposed.[16]

Although it appeared ten years after LMT (as that document had appeared a decade after MCW), MR is not an official production of a territorial bishops' conference. It finds its nearest parallel in the Universa

Laus declaration of 1980, consisting of "points of reference" and "beliefs held in common."[17]

After a preamble offering Christian ritual music as a new way to understand Roman Catholic worship music (arts. 1–9), MR treats music as a language of faith (arts. 10–17), distinguishes between liturgical formation (arts. 18–27) and liturgical preparation (arts. 28–36), analyzes liturgical and musical structures (arts. 37–44), presents textual considerations (arts. 45–55), raises issues associated with cross-cultural music making (arts. 56–63), proposes models of musical leadership (arts. 64–72), examines technology and music (arts. 73–80), and revisits the musical-liturgical-pastoral judgment articulated in MCW (arts. 81–86).

The Snowbird Statement on Catholic Liturgical Music[18]

On 1 November 1995 a group of seventeen musicians and liturgists from the United States, Canada, Ireland, and the United Kingdom issued the "Snowbird Statement on Catholic Liturgical Music" [hereafter SS]. After two consultations held in Utah in the summers of 1992 and 1993, SS was produced under the guidance of the convener of these gatherings, Msgr. M. Francis Mannion, rector of the Cathedral of the Madeleine in Salt Lake City, Utah. Like MR, SS has no authoritative weight comparable to papal, conciliar, curial, or bishops' conference texts. It appears to be addressed to the same audience as MR:

> We seek to contribute in a constructive and respectful spirit to the ongoing discussion of issues which remain controversial, unresolved or even divisive and to engage the wider ecclesial community in advancing the greater good of the church's life in the area of liturgical music [#2]. . . . This statement . . . serves as an affirmation, a critique and a challenge. It does not claim to be conclusive or complete. It is offered as part of a necessary conversation about the future of Catholic worship that must continue with intelligence, wisdom and charity [#28].

Topics treated by SS include theoretical considerations (arts. 3–8), issues of education and formation (arts. 9–14), the practice of liturgical music (arts. 15–25), and the challenge of leadership (arts. 26–27). While some might consider SS as a rejoinder to MR, it is more useful to consider it an independent treatment of some common issues in liturgical music renewal in a North American context.

Having situated the nine documents analyzed in this short study in their historical context, indicated their intended audience, and clarified their authority, we can now trace how they witness to changing understandings of Roman Catholic worship music in the twentieth century.

ENDNOTES

[1] This document appears in two formats: in Italian in *Acta Sanctae Sedis* 36 (1904) 329–39, and in the "official" Latin *("versio fidelis")* in *Acta Apostolicae Sedis* 36 (1904) 387–95. The English translation used in this study is contained in R. F. Hayburn, *Papal Legislation on Sacred Music 95 A.D. to 1977 A.D.* (Collegeville: The Liturgical Press, 1979) 222–31.

Commentaries on the document include: Ilario Alcini, *Pio X e la musica* (Rome: Associazione Italiana de Santa Cecilia, 1956); C. de Brant, "Pius X's *Motu Proprio:* Fifty Years Ago," *Catholic Choirmaster* 39 (1953) 102–6; A. De Santi, "A proposito del *motu proprio* sulla musica sacra," *Civiltà cattolica* 1299 (1904) 278–91; A. Duclos, *Sa Santeté Pie X e la musique religieuse* (Rome: Desclée, 1905); Hayburn, *Papal Legislation,* 195–222; P. Hume, "Music in Church: Pius X's *Motu Proprio,*" *Caecilia* 83 (July–August 1956) 188–90; L. P. Manzetti, "The *Motu Proprio* on Church Music," *Catholic Choirmaster* 1 (February 1915) 5–8; C. P. McNaspy, *The Motu Proprio on Church Music of Pope Pius X: A New Translation and Commentary* (Cincinnati, Ohio: Gregorian Institute of America, 1950); R. J. Schuler, "The *Motu Proprio* and the Progress of Church Music," *Catholic Choirmaster* 39 (1953) 99–101; W.F.P. Stockley, "The Pope and the Reform in Church Music," *American Ecclesiastical Review* 30 (1904) 279–92, 384–401.

For the "pre-history" of the document, see Nancy Ann Stefani, "The Reformation of Catholic Church Music, 1880–1903," thesis (University of Nevada at Reno, 1972).

[2] J. M. Huels, *Liturgical Law: An Introduction,* American Essays in Liturgy, 4 (Washington, D.C.: The Pastoral Press, 1987) 9. Compare the perspective on the force of apostolic letters issued *motu proprio* in R. K. Seasoltz, *New Liturgy, New Laws* (Collegeville: The Liturgical Press, 1980) 174.

[3] The Latin text appears in *Acta Apostolicae Sedis* 48 (1956) 5–25. The English translation used in this study is contained in Hayburn, *Papal Legislation,* 345–56. Commentaries on the document include: Associazione Italiana di Santa Cecilia, *L'enciclica Musicae Sacrae Disciplina de Sua Santità Piuo XII* (Rome: Associazione Italiana di Santa Cecilia per la Musica Sacra, 1957); F. Haberl, "The German High Mass and the Encyclical *Musicae sacrae disciplina,*" *Gregorian Review* 5/2 (March–April 1958) 22–41; F. Romita, "The Encyclical *Musicae sacrae disciplina,*" *Gregorian Review* 4 (July–August 1957) 8–28; J. Schell, "Aesthetische Probleme der Kirchenmusik im Lichte der Enzyklika Pius' XII *Musicae Sacrae Disciplina,*" (dissertation: Berlin, 1961); R. J. Schuler, "The Encyclical *Musicae sacrae disciplina,*" *Caecilia* 84 (1957) 90–94; F. Smith, "Musical Instruments in Church and the Encyclical on Music," *Caecilia* 84 (1957) 237–54.

[4] Most notable are Pius XI's *Divini cultus sanctitatem* of 20 December 1928, which, in reinforcing TLS, calls for its strict observance while clarifying and extending its provisions, and Pius XII's *Mediator Dei* of 20 November 1947, which contains pertinent references to the role of sacred music in its consideration of the nature and purpose of the liturgy in general.

[5] Seasoltz, *New Liturgy,* 172; cf. Huels, *Liturgical Law,* 9.

⁶ The Latin text appears in *Acta Apostolicae Sedis* 50 (1958) 630–63. The English translation used in this study is found in Hayburn, *Papal Legislation,* 356–77.

Commentaries on the document include: F. Antonelli, "Commentary," *Worship* 32/10 (1958) 626–37; F. A. Brunner, "The New Instruction on Sacred Music and Liturgy," *Caecilia* 83 (Fall 1958) 378–81; I. Kelly, "The New Decree on Sacred Music and the Liturgy," *Gregorian Review* 5 (November–December 1958) 10–12; J. Loew, "The New Instruction," *Worship* 33/1 (1958) 2–13; A. G. Martimort and F. Picard, *Liturgie et Musique: traduction de l'Instruction De Musica sacra et sacra Liturgia, 3 septembre 1958,* Lex Orandi, 28 (Paris: Cerf, 1959); T. Richstatter, *Liturgical Law Today: New Style, New Spirit* (Chicago: Franciscan Herald Press, 1977) 41–48.

Of special interest is J. F. Mytych, *Digest of Church Law on Sacred Music* (Toledo, Ohio: Gregorian Institute of America, 1959), which analyzes legislation on Roman Catholic worship music from TLS though 1958Inst.

⁷ Seasoltz, *New Liturgy,* 174–5; cf. Huels, *Liturgical Law,* 9–10.

⁸ The Latin text appears in *Acta Apostolicae Sedis* 56 (1964) 97–138. The English translation used in this study is contained in International Commission on English in the Liturgy, *Documents on the Liturgy 1963–1979: Conciliar, Papal, and Curial Texts* [hereafter DOL] (Collegeville: The Liturgical Press, 1982) nos. 1–131, pp. 4–27.

Commentaries on this document include: Akademie für Musik und darstellend Kunst, *Die Kirchenmusik und das II. vatikanische Konzil* (Graz: Styria, 1965); *The Liturgy of Vatican II: A Symposium in Two Volumes,* ed. W. Baraúna, 2 vols. (Chicago: Franciscan Herald Press, 1966); *The Commentary on the Constitution and on the Instruction on the Sacred Liturgy,* ed. A. Bugnini and C. Braga; trans. V. Mallon (New York: Benziger Bros., 1965); *Costituzione liturgica "Sacrosanctum Concilium" studi,* ed. Congregazione per il Culto Divino, Bibliotheca "Ephemerides Liturgicae" "Subsidia," 38 (Roma: CLV Edizioni Liturgiche, 1986); *La Costituzione sulla sacra liturgia: Genesi storico-dottrinale. Texto latino e traduzione italiana. Esposizione e commento. Norme di applicazione. Riforma liturgica nel mondo,* Collana Magisterio Conciliare, 14 (Torino-Leumann: Elle Di Ci, 1967); E. J. Lengeling, *Die Konstitution des Zweiten Vatikanischen Konzils über die heilige Liturgie,* Lebendiger Gottesdienst, 5–6 (Münster: Regensberg, 1965); *La Maison-Dieu* 77 (1964) [entire issue]; F. McManus, *Sacramental Liturgy* (New York: Herder and Herder, 1967); H. Schmidt, *Die Konstitution über die heilige Liturgie: Texte-Vorgeschichte-Kommentar,* Herder-Taschenbuch, 218 (Freiburg: Herder, 1965); *Commentary on the Documents of Vatican II,* ed. H. Vorgrimler; trans. L. Adolphus, 5 vols. (New York: Herder, 1967) 1.1–87.

⁹ Seasoltz, *New Liturgy,* 170.

¹⁰ Frederick R. McManus, *Liturgical Participation: An Ongoing Assessment,* American Essays in Liturgy, 10 (Washington, D.C.: The Pastoral Press, 1988) 9.

¹¹ The Latin text appears in *Acta Apostolicae Sedis* 59 (1967) 300–20. The English translation used in this study is contained in DOL, nos. 4122–90, pp. 1293–306.

Commentaries on this document include: J. D. Crichton, "The Instruction on Church Music," *Liturgy* 36 (July 1967) 57–63; E. Jaschinski, *Musica sacra oder Musik im Gottesdienst? die Enstehung der Aussagen über die Kirchenmusik in der Liturgiekonstitution "Sacrosanctum Concilium" (1963) und bis zur Instruktion "Musicam Sacram" (1967),* Studien zur Pastoralliturgie, 8 (Regensburg: F. Pustet, 1990); J. M. Joncas, "Re-Reading *Musicam Sacram:* Twenty-Five Years of Development in Roman Rite Liturgical Music," *Worship* 66/2 (May 1992) 212–31; A. Milner, "The Instruction on Sacred Music," *Worship* 41 (June–July 1967) 322–33.

[12] The 1983 text of this document used in this study appears in *The Liturgy Documents: A Parish Resource* [hereafter TLD], 3rd ed. (Chicago: Liturgy Training Publications, 1991) 274–93.

Commentaries on the document include: *Music in Catholic Worship (Revised Edition): The NPM Commentary,* ed. Virgil C. Funk (Washington, D.C.: The Pastoral Press, 1983).

[13] Huels, *Liturgical Law,* 9.

[14] The text of this document used in this study appears in TLD, 295–312.

Commentaries on the document include: R. F. Krisman, "Recent legislation concerning liturgical music in the Roman Catholic Church," *Hymn* 37/1 (1986) 13–14; E. J. McKenna, "Review of *Liturgical Music Today,*" *Worship* 57 (1983) 264–7.

[15] This document appears as Archdiocese of Milwaukee, *The Milwaukee Symposia for Church Composers: A Ten-Year Report* (Washington, D.C./Chicago: The Pastoral Press/Liturgy Training Publications, 1992).

[16] MR, 1–2.

[17] An English translation of this document with introduction, commentary, and glossary is contained in C. Duchesneau and M. Veuthey, *Music and Liturgy: The Universa Laus Document and Commentary,* trans. P. Inwood (Washington, D.C.: Pastoral Press, 1992).

[18] This document appears as *The Snowbird Statement on Catholic Liturgical Music* (Salt Lake City, Utah: The Madeleine Institute, 1995).

What Is Roman Catholic Worship Music?

We begin our analysis by exploring how these nine papal, conciliar, curial, bishops' conference, and collaborative scholarly documents
answer the question: "What is Roman Catholic worship music?"[1] Sub-
questions include: What terminology does the document use for
Roman Catholic worship music? How is Roman Catholic worship
music categorized? What languages are permitted for Roman Catholic
worship music? Are particular styles of worship music encouraged or
forbidden in Roman Catholic worship?

Tra le sollecitudini

TLS divides music intended for use in the worship of the Roman
Rite into three categories. In first place is Gregorian chant:

> 3. . . . Gregorian chant . . . is . . . the proper chant of the Roman
> Church, the only chant which she has inherited from the ancient Fathers,
> which she has jealously kept for so many centuries in her liturgical books,
> which she offers to the faithful as her own music, which she insists on
> being used exclusively in some parts of her liturgy, and which, lastly, has
> been so happily restored to its original perfection and purity by recent
> study.

Note that although Pius X claims Gregorian chant to be the proper
chant of the Roman *Church*, it would be more accurate to claim it as the
proper chant of the Roman *Rite:* in the West, Ambrosian and
Mozarabic chant are proper to the Milanese and Spanish rites respec-
tively, and each of the Eastern Rites has likewise developed its own
proper chant. Great emphasis is placed on Gregorian chant's longevity:
part of its value for Roman Rite worship is that it serves a means by

13

which contemporary Roman Rite worshipers can be united to those who have gone before them in faith in using the same music. (Contemporary scholarship posits that, in spite of legends ascribing this music to Pope Gregory the Great, Gregorian chant arises from the interaction of Roman and Frankish worship music during the Carolingian period; a presumed earlier "old Roman" chant, genuinely proper to the worship of the city of Rome, is extant in a few manuscripts.)[2] Pius X also makes reference to the musicological work of the monks of Solesmes, both in investigating the manuscript sources for the chant and in developing theories about its proper performance.

In second place is "classical polyphony":

> 4. . . . Music of the classical school, especially . . . that of the Roman school, which reached its greatest perfection in the sixteenth century under Pierluigi da Palestrina, and which afterwards went on producing excellent liturgical compositions . . . agrees very well with the highest model of all sacred music, namely Gregorian chant, and therefore it deserves, together with Gregorian chant, to be used in the more solemn offices of the Church.

Although historians of the musical life of Europe tend to use the term "classical" to refer to the compositions produced in the era of Haydn, Mozart, and the early Beethoven, Pius X uses the term to refer to unaccompanied vocal music employing multiple vocal lines; it is distinguished from chant by the fact that it is written in parts rather than being monodic, although its tonal organization seems to be modal as is the chant.

More modern music appears in third place:

> 5. . . . More modern music may also be allowed in churches, since it has produced compositions good and serious and dignified enough to be worthy of liturgical use. Nevertheless, since modern music has become chiefly a secular art, greater care must be taken, when admitting it, that nothing profane be allowed, nothing that is reminiscent of theatrical pieces, nothing based as to its form on the style of secular compositions.

What seems to distinguish more modern music (namely Western European composition from the sixteenth through the dawn of the twentieth century) from chant and classical polyphony is the use of instrumental accompaniment, tonal organization by keys rather than modes, and chordal in addition to polyphonic choral style. Note Pius X's reticence in using this music, since he judges it to be primarily secular in orientation; his confident division of music into sacred and secular categories and his horror of theatrical music in Roman Catholic worship will be treated in chapter three.

In addition to this threefold categorization by style, TLS further specifies Roman Rite worship music by language:

> 7. The language of the Roman Church is Latin. It is therefore forbidden to sing anything in the vulgar tongue during solemn liturgical functions, and much more is it forbidden to sing in the vulgar tongue the parts, either proper or common, of the Mass and the Office.

While texts in Latin form the bulk of those employed in the Roman Rite, in fact both Hebrew (e.g., Amen, Alleluia) and Greek (e.g., Kyrie eleison, Hagios ho theos) also appear. Thus for Pius X genuine Roman Rite worship music must be performed in the languages used by the official liturgical books; even strict translations of these texts into the vernacular would be unacceptable for the *missa cantata:*

> 8. Since the text to be sung and the order in which it is to be sung are already determined for every liturgical service, it is not lawful to change either the words or their order, nor to substitute another text, nor to leave anything out, either entirely or in part, except in the cases in which the rubrics allow the organ alone to replace certain verses which must then be recited in the choir. It is only allowed, according to the custom of the Roman Church, to sing a Motet in honor of the Blessed Sacrament after the *Benedictus* at high Mass. A short Motet with words approved by the Church may also be added after the proper Offertory of the Mass has been sung.
>
> 9. The liturgical text must be sung just as it stands in the authentic books, without changing or transposing the words, without needless repetition, without dividing the syllables, and always so that it can be understood by the people who hear it.

Musicae sacrae disciplina

MSD modifies some of the assertions made in TLS, nuancing Pius X's pronouncements and offering a new categorization scheme. First, where TLS claimed Gregorian chant as the worship music proper to the Roman *Church*, MSD recognizes it as proper to the Roman *Rite*:

> 50. It is quite obvious that what We have said briefly here about Gregorian chant applies mainly to the Latin Roman Rite of the Church. It can also, however, be applied to a certain extent to the liturgical chants of other rites—either to those of the West, such as the Ambrosian, Gallican or Mozarabic, or to the various Eastern rites.

The respect shown here for the liturgical and musical traditions of other rites will be confirmed in SC.

Second, in treating TLS's second category of Roman Rite worship music (classical polyphony), MSD acknowledges both musicological advances in restoring polyphonic liturgical compositions and the work of certain "Caecilian" composers who, rather than employing the musical resources and styles of their contemporary colleagues, have deliberately written in the style of sixteenth-century Roman polyphony:

> 54. Although over the course of the centuries genuine polyphonic art gradually declined and profane melodies often crept into it, during recent decades the indefatigable labors of experts have brought about a restoration. The works of the old composers have been carefully studied and proposed as models to be imitated and rivalled by modern composers.

Third, MSD continues TLS's suspicion of post-sixteenth-century musical styles as appropriate for Roman Rite worship. Pius X's horror of theatrical music at liturgy has led to the articulation of further criteria for determining appropriate worship music:

> 57. Great prudence and care should be used in this serious matter [of modern music] in order to keep out of churches polyphonic music which, because of its heavy and bombastic style, might obscure the sacred words of the liturgy by a kind of exaggeration, interfere with the conduct of the liturgical service, or, finally, lower the skill and competence of the singers to the disadvantage of sacred worship.

Fourth, and perhaps most importantly, MSD acknowledges another category of Roman Rite worship music: popular religious hymns. (Some commentators have suggested that Pius XII's diplomatic experience in Germany exposed him to the vigorous hymn-singing traditions of that country, an experience that transformed his opinion of the religious value of such singing.) While lauding the intimate connection between faith and culture represented in such popular hymn-singing, MSD restricts its use at the *missa solemnis;* there all the music sung must have texts in Latin, Greek, or Hebrew found in the liturgical books, except for specifically identified vernacular pieces hallowed by custom (e.g., a vernacular hymn sung after the eucharistic consecration in some areas of Germany). In a decision of far-reaching consequences, the document approves the use of vernacular hymnody at the *missa lecta,* thus giving official recognition to the entrance hymn, offertory hymn, communion hymn, exit hymn pattern familiar to many U.S. worshiping communities. It is clear, however, that MSD does not consider such vernacular singing as genuinely liturgical music, but as popular devotional singing *coordinated with* the liturgical action. An unfortunate consequence of this practice is that elements of comparatively lesser theological-ritual weight are given undue prominence in congregational song while the most important elements (e.g., the Sanctus and the Amen concluding the Roman Canon) are recited. Nevertheless vernacular singing during the liturgy is here officially recognized as a possibility for the entire Roman Rite and not just by indult for particular territories:

> 62. Besides those things that are intimately associated with the Church's sacred liturgy, there are also popular religious hymns which derive their origin from the liturgical chant itself. Most of these are written in the language of the people. Since those are closely related to the mentality and temperament of individual national groups, they differ considerably among themselves according to the character of different races and localities.

> 64. Such hymns cannot be used in Solemn High Masses without the express permission of the Holy See. Nevertheless at Masses that are not sung solemnly these hymns can be a powerful aid in keeping the faithful from attending the Holy Sacrifice like dumb and idle spectators. They can help to make the faithful accompany the sacred services both mentally and vocally and to join their own piety to the prayers of the priest. This happens when these hymns are properly adapted to the individual parts of the Mass.

The 1958 Instruction

Following the lead of MSD, 1958Inst acknowledges Gregorian chant, polyphony, modern sacred music, and popular religious singing as categories of Roman Rite worship music. In addition two new categories appear: "4. By 'sacred music' is meant: a. Gregorian chant; b. sacred polyphony; c. modern sacred music; d. sacred organ music; e. popular religious singing; f. religious music."

1958Inst's treatment of the chant, polyphony, and modern sacred music repeats and summarizes the teaching of TLS and MSD:

> 5. The "Gregorian chant" used in liturgical functions is the sacred chant of the Roman Church and is to be found for liturgical use in various books approved by the Holy See, piously and faithfully copied from ancient and venerable tradition or composed in recent times on the pattern of ancient tradition. Of its nature Gregorian chant does not require the accompaniment of an organ or other musical instrument.

> 6. By "sacred polyphony" is meant that measured song which, derived from the motifs of Gregorian chant and composed with many parts, without instrumental accompaniment, began to flourish in the Latin Church in the Middle Ages. Giovanni Pierluigi da Palestrina (1525–1594) was its principal promoter in the second half of the sixteenth century and today it is promoted by illustrious masters of that art.

7. "Modern sacred music" is music which has many parts, does not exclude instrumental accompaniment, and is composed in accord with the progress of musical art. When this is intended specifically for liturgical use, it must be pious and preserve a religious character. On this condition it is accepted in liturgical service.

1958Inst's discussion of popular religious song seems to expand upon MSD's treatment in three ways. First, this culture-specific religious music is no longer limited to hymns as in MSD; apparently 1958Inst recognizes that there are cultures which produce popular religious singing that does not fit the European model of hymnody. Second, 1958Inst does not claim, as did MSD, that popular religious hymns arise from chant; while some vernacular hymns may be translations or paraphrases of pieces in the chant repertoire, other popular religious singing may find its inspiration in other textual sources (e.g., the Bible, religious poetry). Third, 1958Inst seems to shift the understanding of "universal" from its usage in TLS. In Pius X's thinking what was universal was a particular repertoire of music (Gregorian chant) that was equally at home in all cultures; in 1958Inst what is universal is not a particular repertoire, but the human instinct to express religious feeling with musical means:

9. "Popular religious singing" is that which springs spontaneously from that religious sentiment with which human beings have been endowed by the Creator himself. For this reason, it is universal and flourishes among all peoples.

Since this song is very suitable for imbuing the private and social life of the faithful with a Christian spirit, it was cultivated in the Church as far back as the most ancient times . . . , and is recommended today for arousing the piety of the faithful and for giving beauty to pious exercises. Sometimes it can even be permitted in liturgical functions themselves.

In addition to these four categories of vocal worship music, 1958Inst recognizes a category of nonvocal worship music. The emphasis still remains on the contribution an instrument can make in accompanying singing, but its gift of producing nontexted musical sound during worship is also recognized. There is evidence that organs, associated in antiquity with the theater and raucous in their sound production, were forbidden as accompaniment instruments for Christian worship. Thus the document notes that a connection between organ playing and the liturgy could only have developed once the instrument itself had been shorn of its theatrical connotations and been developed technologically enough to serve as a reliable accompanying instrument:

8. "Sacred organ music" is music composed solely for the organ. Ever since the pipe organ came into use as a most suitable accompaniment, this has been developed by illustrious masters. If the laws of sacred music are scrupulously observed, organ music can greatly contribute to the beauty of the sacred liturgy.

Finally 1958Inst describes a category of music unsuitable for use during worship in the Roman Rite, although it may evoke religious sentiments:

10. By "religious music" is meant any music which, either because of the intention of the composer or because of the subject and purpose of the composition, is likely to express and arouse pious and religious sentiments and is therefore "most helpful to religion.". . . But, since it is not meant for sacred worship and is expressed in a rather free form, it is not permitted in liturgical functions.

What is most interesting about this article is the appearance of further criteria to determine genuine worship music: the composer's intention (was the music specifically intended for Roman Rite worship or merely imported into it from another social setting?), the subject and purpose of the composition (was the music intended to evoke Roman Rite worship or to represent a general religious quest?) and propriety of form (was the music bound to the ritual action or intended to be played "for its own sake"?).

Inst1958 reinforces MSD's teaching on the use of vernacular songs during Roman Rite worship. It distinguishes between *liturgical worship* and *pious exercises:* the proper language for the former is what is found in the liturgical books, while the latter may also use various vernaculars. It also distinguishes between *direct* liturgical participation (in which one sings or recites texts in the language found in the liturgical books) and *indirect* liturgical participation (in which one sings or recites texts in the vernacular while the ministers employ the languages of the liturgical books):

13. a. Latin is the language of liturgical functions, unless the . . . liturgical books (either general or specific ones) explicitly permit another language. . . .

b. In sung liturgical functions no liturgical text translated verbatim in the vernacular may be sung except by special permission. . . .

c. Special exceptions granted by the Holy See from this law on the exclusive use of Latin in liturgical functions remain in force, but one may not give them a broader interpretation or transfer them to other regions without authorization from the Holy See.

d. In pious exercises, any language may be used which is convenient to the faithful.

14. a. In sung Masses, the Latin language must be used not only by the priest celebrant and the ministers, but also by the choir and the faithful. . . .

b. In a *read* Mass, the priest celebrant, his ministers and the faithful who participate directly in the liturgical functions with the celebrant must pronounce in a clear voice those parts of the Mass which apply to them and may use only the Latin language.

Then, if the faithful wish to add some popular prayers or hymns to this *direct* liturgical participation, according to local custom, this may be done in the vernacular.

Although the following prescriptions do not apply strictly to the use of the vernacular in sung Roman Rite worship, they do hint at what was being done in some more "progressive" communities during this period, experiments in liturgical participation that will find confirmation at the Vatican Council II:

[14.] c. It is strictly forbidden to say aloud the parts of the Proper, Ordinary and Canon of the Mass together with the priest celebrant, in Latin or in translation, and this applies either to the faithful or to a commentator. . . .

It is desirable that in read Masses on Sundays and feastdays, the Gospel and Epistle be read by a lector in the vernacular for the convenience of the faithful.

Sacrosanctum Concilium

SC does not offer a formal definition of Roman Catholic worship music, but affirms its preeminence among the arts associated with worship. Genuine worship music is not simply an auxiliary prop to the liturgical action, but the very means by which certain liturgical actions occur:

112. The musical tradition of the universal Church is a treasure of inestimable value, greater even than that of any other art. The main reason for this preeminence is that, as sacred song closely bound to the text, it forms a necessary or integral part of the solemn liturgy.

Note that the document does not claim that Roman Rite worship cannot take place without music. Rather music forms a necessary component of the *solemn* liturgy (e.g., for the Eucharist, this would include the *missa solemnis* and the *missa cantata,* but not the *missa lecta*). The contribution music makes to worship cannot be replaced by any other art form, but is not strictly indispensable for Roman Rite worship.

We have observed an increasingly precise differentiation of Roman Rite worship music in the documents studied so far, from the tripartite categorization of TLS through the quadripart categorization of MSD to the quintuple categorization of 1958Inst. These distinctions disappear in SC. Instead the Constitution on the Sacred Liturgy presents only two fundamental categories: Gregorian chant and all other music, including both polyphony and popular religious singing:

> 116. The Church acknowledges Gregorian chant as distinctive of the Roman liturgy; therefore, other things being equal, it should be given pride of place in liturgical services.

> But other kinds of sacred music, especially polyphony, are by no means excluded from liturgical celebrations, provided they accord with the spirit of the liturgical service. . . .

> 118. The people's own religious songs are to be encouraged with care so that in sacred devotions as well as during services of the liturgy itself, in keeping with the rubrical norms and requirements, the faithful may raise their voices in song.

Perhaps the greatest change in Roman Rite worship music permitted by SC is in the use of the vernacular. While asserting that the use of the Latin language is to be preserved in the Latin rites, article 36 allows, when it would be advantageous to the people, the use of the vernacular in parts of the liturgy, especially "the readings, instructions, and certain prayers and chants." Territorial bishops' conferences are given the authority to determine the extent of vernacular liturgical usage and to approve translations intended for use in Roman Rite worship. Article 54 applies this general permission to the celebration of the Eucharist: although the faithful should be able "to say or sing together those parts of the Ordinary of the Mass belonging to them," the readings, the general intercessions, and the "parts belonging to the people" might all be executed in the vernacular. Article 63 applies the prescriptions of article 36 to the celebration of the other sacraments and sacramentals. While envisioning that clerics would continue to celebrate the Liturgy of the Hours in Latin, article 101 permits the Divine Office to be prayed in the vernacular by monks and nuns bound to its celebration, as well as clerics for whom "the use of Latin would constitute a grave difficulty." The permissions granted by these articles extend not only to recited but also to sung texts:

> 113. As regards the language to be used, the provisions of art. 36 are to be observed; for the Mass, those of art. 54; for the sacraments, those of art. 63; for the divine office, those of art. 101.

Since the use of prescribed Latin, Greek, and Hebrew texts no longer serves to identify genuine Roman Rite liturgical music in contrast to the music of "pious exercises," SC sketches some criteria by which this music can be evaluated:

> 121. The texts intended to be sung must always be consistent with Catholic teaching; indeed they should be drawn chiefly from holy Scripture and from liturgical sources.

It should be clear that these criteria apply only to worship music intended to be sung with texts; they give no guidance for purely instrumental music at liturgy. Nor does SC indicate who will be competent to determine if the texts sung are consistent with Catholic teaching.

Musicam Sacram

In offering a taxonomy of Roman Rite worship music, MS reminds one of its predecessor, 1958Inst:

> 4. a. Music is "sacred" insofar as it is composed for the celebration of divine worship and possesses integrity of form.
>
> b. The term "sacred music" here includes: Gregorian chant, the several styles of polyphony, both ancient and modern, sacred music for organ and for other permitted instruments, and the sacred, i.e., liturgical or religious, music of the people.

Note that the terminology of sacred music, found in Roman documents from TLS on, is retained. Where SC had categorized Roman Rite worship music in terms of sung texts as "Gregorian chant" and "everything else," MS offers a four-fold categorization. Gregorian chant retains the premiere position, but polyphony is no longer divided on the basis of whether or not it is instrumentally accompanied (presumably choral music in vernacular languages would be included in this category), nontexted instrumental music is acknowledged as part of Roman Rite worship music, and popular religious singing (whether as hymns or in other forms) is also recognized.

MS presumes that Roman Rite worshipers will offer sung worship in both a Latin and a vernacular repertoire:

> 47. . . . Pastors are to see to it that, in addition to the vernacular, "the faithful are also able to say or to sing together in Latin those parts of the Ordinary of the Mass belonging to them."
>
> 48. Once the vernacular has been introduced into the Mass, local Ordinaries should determine whether it is advisable to retain one or more Masses in Latin, particularly sung Masses. This applies especially to great

cities in churches with a large attendance of faithful using a foreign language. . . .

50. In liturgies celebrated in Latin:

a. Because it is proper to the Roman liturgy, Gregorian chant has pride of place, all other things being equal. Proper use should be made of the melodies in the *editiones typicae* of this chant.

b. "It is desirable also that an edition be prepared containing simpler melodies for use in small churches" (SC).

c. Other kinds of melodies, either for unison or part-singing and taken from the traditional repertoire or from new works, are to be held in respect, encouraged, and used as the occasion suggests.

51. In view of local conditions, the pastoral good of the faithful, and the idiom of each language, parish priests (pastors) are to decide whether selections from the musical repertoire composed for Latin texts should be used not only for liturgies in Latin but also for those in the vernacular. But there is nothing opposed to celebrations which mix the use of Latin and the various vernacular languages.

These prescriptions of MS apply SC's directives to concrete situations. First, the document suggests that each diocese will retain a Lord's Day Eucharist celebrated at least once a week in Latin in a major church, a celebration that would certainly include Gregorian chant and possibly unaccompanied polyphony and/or accompanied choral music. This celebration is especially intended for pastoral purposes: visitors from other cultures who might be excluded from a vernacular celebration should be able to worship with the texts and music of the Latin liturgy. Second, the document clarifies that Gregorian chant holds pride of place *for liturgies celebrated in Latin:* when a community celebrates in Latin using the reformed texts and *ordo Missae* of the *Missale Romanum*, Gregorian chant is the preferred music with which to render the texts, although unaccompanied polyphony and accompanied choral music are not forbidden. Third, unlike earlier prescriptions that limited vernacular singing to the *missa lecta* and forbade it at the *missa cantata* and *missa solemnis*, MS approves a range of texts for worship music in a single celebration: celebrations may be all in Latin, Greek, or Hebrew, all in the vernacular, or may mix traditional and vernacular languages in any proportion.

Music in Catholic Worship

Although in quoting SC 112, MCW seems to limit Roman Rite worship music to vocal rendering of texts, the document places this music in the category of signs and symbols:

> 23. Among the many signs and symbols used by the Church to celebrate its faith, music is of preeminent importance. As sacred song united to words it forms a necessary or integral part of the solemn liturgy. . . . [Cf. CS 112.]

To present worship music as significant communication or as symbolic interaction opens new avenues of approach to understanding it. Many contemporary theologians have distinguished between signs as pointers to an absent reality and symbols as a means by which reality manifests itself. They speak of the humanity of Christ as the sacramental symbol of God, the Church as the sacramental symbol of Christ, the sacraments as sacramental symbols of the Church, etc.[3]

MCW does not present worship music so much as a modality of divine communication as the means by which the Church celebrates its faith. The document does not deny that a divine-human dialogue may take place through musical signs and symbols, but the emphasis is clearly on the horizontal dimension of worship music, the significant and symbolic self-expression of the worshiping assembly.

To affirm that music functions as sign and symbol in worship is to heighten its importance in the worship event. Just as an analysis of a painting cannot substitute for gazing upon it, just as a synopsis of a novel cannot supplant reading it, so reciting texts intended to be sung in worship cannot engage worshipers in the same way as singing them. This perspective leads MCW to underline the importance of music in every experience of worship:

> 24. . . . Ideally, every communal celebration of faith, including funerals and the sacraments of baptism, confirmation, penance, anointing, and matrimony, should include music and singing. Where it is possible to celebrate the Liturgy of the Hours in a community, it, too, should include music.

Liturgical Music Today

The stance taken toward Roman Rite worship music in MCW is even more strongly emphasized in LMT:

> 5. These guidelines concern the Church's liturgy, which is inherently musical. If music is not valued within the liturgy, then this statement will have little to offer. On the other hand, if music is appreciated as a necessarily normal dimension of every experience of communal worship, then what follows may help to promote continued understanding of the liturgy, dialogue among those responsible for its implementation, and music itself as sung prayer.

We see here a progression from SC's claim that texted vocal music is a necessary or integral part of the *solemn* liturgy through MCW's assertion that, as part of the symbolic character of worship, music should

ideally be part of every liturgical celebration to LMT's declaration that
the Church's liturgy is *"inherently musical,"* a "necessarily normal dimension of every experience of communal worship." Where earlier
documents spoke of music adorning the liturgy, of serving as the
liturgy's handmaid *(ancilla)*, LMT underlines music as the symbolic
medium through which certain liturgical acts are performed, referring
to it as sung prayer.

Highlighting MS's permission to mix sung languages in a single
celebration, LMT opts for an eclectic approach to choosing repertoire:

> 14. Different languages may be used in the same celebration. [General
> Instruction of the Liturgy of the Hours, 276.] This may also be said of mix-
> ing different musical idioms and media. For example, pastoral reasons
> might suggest that in a given liturgical celebration some music reflect
> classical hymnody, with other music drawn from gospel or "folk" idioms,
> from contemporary service music, or from the plainsong or polyphonic
> repertoires. . . .

> 15. While this principle upholding musical plurality has pastoral value, it
> should never be employed as a license for including poor music. At the
> same time, it needs to be recognized that a certain musical integrity
> within a liturgical prayer or rite can be achieved only by unity in the mu-
> sical composition. . . .

Note some tensions generated by opting for this eclectic approach.
First, although it rejects claims to a global or transcultural standard
against which all music must be judged, LMT presumes that one can
develop criteria for judging the quality of music within individual
styles: just as there can be good or poor classical polyphony, so there
can be good or poor gospel songs. According to LMT, only music
judged good within each idiom is appropriate to Roman Rite worship.
Second, the document hints that more is involved in choosing repertoire than a musical-liturgical-pastoral judgment applied to individual
elements of the liturgy. The micro- and macro-units of the liturgical
event must also be considered.

A signal contribution of LMT is its forthright recognition of the
multicultural dimensions of Roman Rite worship in many sections of
the United States:

> 54. Just as the great liturgical music of the past is to be remembered, cher-
> ished and used, so also the rich diversity of the cultural heritage of the
> many peoples of our country today must be recognized, fostered and
> celebrated. The United States of America is a nation of nations, a country
> in which people speak many tongues, live their lives in diverse ways,
> celebrate events in song and music in the folkways of their cultural, eth-
> nic and racial roots.

55. Liturgical music today <u>must be as diverse and multi-cultural as the</u> <u>members of the assembly.</u> Pastors and musicians must encourage not only the use of traditional music of other languages, but also the composition of new liturgical music appropriate to various cultures. Likewise <u>the great musical gifts of the Hispanic, Black and other ethnic communi-</u> <u>ties in the Church should enrich the whole Church in the United States in</u> <u>a dialogue of cultures.</u>

We see here a progression from Roman Rite worship music being limited to Latin, Greek, and Hebrew texts found in the liturgical books sung in western European idioms, through Roman Rite worship music employing vernacular texts in other musico-cultural idioms, to Roman Rite worship music in a variety of vernaculars and idioms. The central principle seems to be that Roman Rite worship music should reflect the musical and cultural diversity of the people who have actually gathered to celebrate. <u>LMT does not endorse employing the worship</u> <u>music of ethnic groups not physically represented in a given celebra-</u> <u>tion simply for the sake of consciousness-raising.</u>

The Milwaukee Report

MR departs from the earlier terminology employed to refer to Roman Rite worship music. Rather than ecclesiastical, liturgical, religious, or sacred music, it prefers the term Christian ritual music:

6. Until recently the church tended to judge music either as sacred or profane according to standards and criteria that it considered to be objective. . . . From this viewpoint, one can posit the existence of "sacred" or holy music.

A significant departure from this approach, foreshadowed in *Musicae sacrae disciplina,* was made explicit in *Sacrosanctum Concilium* and *Musicam Sacram.* . . . Our document continues this emphasis on music's function in ritual by adopting the more accurate term "Christian ritual music." This term underscores the interconnection between music and the other elements of the rite: distinguishable facets of a single event.

7. The category of Christian ritual music offers new ways to understand and classify the various musical elements in worship. For example, rather than simply focusing on sung texts and listing these according to the liturgical importance of the text, a ritual music perspective allows for other categories encompassing more than liturgical texts alone.

This shift in terminology also signals a shift in categorization. Rather than schematizing Roman Rite worship music on the basis of style (e.g., chant, polyphony, modern music), language (e.g., Latin vs. vernacular), or individual genres (e.g., acclamations, hymns, litanies),

MR proposes a new categorization based on ritual function. In footnote 15 it notes a four-fold schema developed by Edward Foley and Mary McGann:

> One formulation . . . suggests that there are four types of ritual music: 1) music alone, 2) music wed to a ritual action, 3) music united to a text, and 4) music wed to a text, accompanying a ritual action.[4]

MR presumes that the texts for Roman Rite worship music may be in any language; criteria for evaluating such texts will arise from their ritual efficacy. Similarly, no style of music is commended or excluded a priori. Evaluation of style will always revert to determining how well a given style facilitates ritual activity among the participants.

The Snowbird Statement

SS accepts the terminology of "Christian ritual music" appearing in MR, but is cautious about its application:

> 5. We welcome the development of the concept of ritual music among liturgical scholars and musicians. This important development has clarified how intimately music is tied to ritual forms and how problematic liturgical music becomes when it is inadequately formed by the structure and spirit of the liturgy. Yet, the theory and practice of ritual music is often inadequately attentive to the beautiful and the artistic. It often seems to go unnoticed that aesthetically high quality music has the ability to make rituals more powerful and more engaging. Unfortunately, much ritual music in the Catholic church today is hampered by an excessive academicism and an artless rationality. In this regard, the concept of ritual music is very much a product of modernity and, as such, is already showing its age and transitional character. We call for further development in the concept and practice of ritual music so as to avoid utilitarian functionalism and to advance a liturgical music practice that is beautiful and artistically well-formed.

In the light of these assertions it is probably significant that SS presents itself as a statement on "Catholic liturgical music" rather than "Christian ritual music."

SS does not espouse any clear schema for categorizing Roman Catholic worship music, whether by style, language, genre, or ritual function. It acknowledges the propriety of employing chant in Roman Catholic worship, but does not claim it as normative:

> 21. In view of the growing interest in Gregorian chant among people of diverse backgrounds and ages, we encourage the rediscovery of the role of chant in Catholic worship. The modern use of this chant is provided

for in the *Graduale Simplex, Jubilate Deo,* the *Gregorian Missal* and other sources. Whether in Latin or in the vernacular, chant connects the modern liturgy with its ancient roots and can provide a source of unity for multicultural and multilingual worship, speaking to and from the collective musical consciousness of the church. Among the most successful examples today of common sung prayer are the chant versions of the Lord's Prayer, *Kyrie eleison* and *Agnus Dei,* litanies and simple hymns. Moreover, melodic cells and motifs drawn from the church's collective memory can also serve as a basis for evocative modern composition.

(Interestingly SS refers to chant "in the vernacular," presumably meaning unaccompanied monody modally organized without regularly recurring metrical organization set to vernacular texts.)

SS also recognizes choral music as appropriate to Roman Rite worship, although it does not employ the earlier distinctions between "classical polyphony" and "more modern music":

22. We affirm the use of choral music from the church's heritage, including Gregorian chant and polyphony, as recommended by various church documents of and since the Second Vatican Council. Liturgically sound criteria, however, must inform the use of the heritage of music. Pieces from the so-called treasury of sacred music must not be used in an unreformed, preconciliar manner, for reasons of mere nostalgic sentimentality or in any way at cross-purposes with the structure and pastoral intent of the reformed rites. Rather, the church's heritage of sacred music (which today certainly includes treasures from other Christian musical traditions) must be used with careful attention to the structure of the reformed liturgy, with a well-informed sense for how a rite unfolds, and with respect for pastoral needs and sensibilities. A discerning use of traditional music can be a spiritually edifying enhancement of liturgical celebrations and a sign of our union with and indebtedness to our forebears. The treasury of sacred music should not be understood as closed, however. It can function as a wellspring, guide and inspiration for future composition. It can also serve to foster organic growth and continued creativity in Catholic liturgical music.

SS's recognition of Roman Rite Church music repertoire including "treasures from other Christian musical traditions" raises the question of criteria by which one could judge which pieces, genres, and styles of worship music generated for other worship heritages may be imported into and grafted on Roman Rite liturgical worship. For example, can *Ein Feste Burg* be shorn of its traditionally anti-Catholic connotations and sung in Roman Rite worship? Are Anglican chant patterns sung by schola or choir appropriate musical vehicles for the responsorial psalm in the Roman Rite Liturgy of the Word that seems to presume either a purely choral gradual or a responsorial chant shared between cantor and assembly? Are witness and testimony songs characteristic of what James White has termed "frontier" worship appropriate in Roman Rite worship?

Perhaps connected to its call for "detailed study of successful patterns [of congregational singing] in other Christian churches" (art. 9), SS makes a strong case that hymnody should be considered a significant component of Roman Rite worship music:

> 19. We call for a positive approach to hymnody in the Roman liturgy and the development of criteria for the appropriate use of hymnody in all liturgical rites. The tradition of Catholic hymnody stretches back to congregational office hymns of the early church; includes sequences of the medieval eucharistic liturgy which in effect were strophic hymns; and extends through vernacular medieval community hymn singing which was well developed before the Reformation. The use of hymnody, already a feature of preconciliar eucharistic and devotional services, has continued to grow since the Vatican Council II and deserves today stronger encouragement.
>
> The hymn represents a poetically generative form of time-tested value for stimulating congregational participation. Well-crafted new hymn texts serve to amplify lectionary themes and bring spiritual enrichment to the hymn-singing tradition. Strophic hymnody, a well-established part of the religious culture of the English-speaking world, may rightly be seen as an authentic expression of liturgical inculturation. Hymnody is also ecumenically important as a musical bond between various Christian traditions.
>
> We acknowledge that the hymn form poses certain challenges in relating well to the ritual and textual structure of the eucharist, but we reject the view that hymnody is intrinsically incompatible with the eucharistic liturgy. The task at hand is to advance the liturgical use of hymns, even if critically, and to clarify when and how hymns might be used appropriately in Catholic worship.

No restrictions on the languages of the texts to be sung in Roman Rite worship appears in SS but, as will be noted in chapter three, particular styles are judged to be incompatible with its worship.

With MR's and SS's emphasis on worship music serving ritual functions in Christian liturgy, we are led to consider the purpose(s) of worship music in general, the subject of our next chapter.

ENDNOTES

[1] "Various terms have emerged over the centuries for designating the music employed in the church's worship. The most common of these are: church music, liturgical music, religious music and sacred music. . . . The an-

cient designation church music (*musica ecclesiastica*) has come to denote virtu-
ally any music employed within worship during the history of the Christian
churches. . . . Liturgical music (*musica liturgica*) is a more recent formulation
. . . which came to prominence in the 1960s as a specific term for music integral to the reformed liturgy of the Roman Catholic church after the Second
Vatican Council. . . . Religious music (*musica religiosa*) currently serves as a
popular label for any music that is perceived to have an explicit or implicit religious theme. . . . Sacred music (*musica sacra*) is at once the preferred term in
universal documents of the Roman Catholic church for music composed for
'the celebration of divine worship' . . . yet in common usage is a generic term
for religious music, especially that which is considered art music." E. Foley,
"Liturgical Music," *The New Dictionary of Sacramental Worship*, ed. P. E. Fink
(Collegeville: The Liturgical Press, 1990) 854–5. For other terminological discussions, see: C. Duchesneau, "Musique sacrée, musique d'église, musique
liturgique: changement de mentalité?" *Notitiae* 23 (1987) 1189–99; N. Schalz,
"'Musique sacrée': naissance et évolution d'un concept," *La Maison-Dieu* 164
(1985) 87–104; idem, "La notion de 'Musique sacrée'—une tradition récente,"
La Maison-Dieu 108 (1971) 32–57.

In the light of the above distinctions I have chosen to label what I am investigating as "Roman Catholic worship music," i.e., music intended for use
in Roman Catholic (primarily Roman Rite) worship, both liturgical (in celebrations of the sacraments, sacramentals, and the Liturgy of the Hours) and
nonliturgical (in popular devotions).

[2] "Gregory's actual share in its composition, or the regulation of its liturgical use, has been much debated. Since there is a gap of nearly three centuries
between Gregory's life and the appearance of the first completely notated
chant-books, it is unlikely that what finally entered the written musical record
is what Gregory knew, even if we subtract the chants for those days whose
liturgies were added to the calendar after Gregory's time. It is nevertheless
possible to argue that an ancient core of the repertory, in something very much
like the state in which we find it in the late ninth century, might date back to
Gregory. The arguments are circumstantial, for we have no reliable contemporary witnesses to any musical activity on Gregory's part, and must rely on in-
ferences drawn from the date of the texts and the style of the music. More
difficulty arises from the fact that the very idea of Gregory as a composer cannot be traced back earlier than the eighth century, although there are pieces of
evidence that some chants may very well be as old as Gregory's time. . . .

"The events that led to the establishment of the chant repertory we know
as 'Gregorian' are inextricably bound up with political developments of the
eighth century, principally the establishment of a strong and extensive
Frankish kingdom, which by the end of the reign of Charlemagne (768–814)
covered an area corresponding to that of modern France, West Germany, and
north and central Italy. . . . Charlemagne was deeply concerned that the
church in his domain would follow the liturgy according to Roman practice,
as far as possible, which naturally included the plainchant of the liturgy. . . .

"Old Roman chant . . . serves the same liturgy as Gregorian chant, but
without the liturgical modifications made by the Franks in the eighth and

ninth centuries. That means that for the majority of chants in the Roman liturgy, both an Old Roman and a Gregorian version exist. . . . The principal sources of the Old Roman melodies are three graduals . . . and two antiphoners." David Hiley, *Western Plainchant: A Handbook* (Oxford: Clarendon Press, 1993) 503–4, 514, 531.

[3] For a concise summary of these views see Herbert Vorgrimler, "The Sacramental Theology of Salvation," *Sacramental Theology,* trans. Linda M. Maloney (Collegeville: The Liturgical Press, 1992) 27–42.

[4] For further discussion of this schema see E. Foley and M. McGann, *Music and the Eucharistic Prayer* (Collegeville: The Liturgical Press, 1988).

2

What Is the Purpose of Roman Catholic Worship Music?

We have seen how the nine documents under investigation vary in their understanding of what constitutes Roman Catholic worship music, the terminology used to refer to it, and the criteria employed to determine its proper language and style. In this chapter we will explore how these documents present the purpose of Roman Catholic worship music and what functions support this purpose.

Tra le sollecitudini

The very first article of TLS sets the direction for twentieth-century discussions of the purpose of worship music in the Roman Rite:

> 1. Sacred music, being an integral part of the liturgy, is directed to the general object of this liturgy, namely, the glory of God and the sanctification and edification of the faithful. It helps to increase the beauty and splendor of the ceremonies of the Church, and since its chief duty is to clothe the liturgical text, which is presented to the understanding of the faithful, with suitable melody, its object is to make that text more efficacious, so that the faithful may through this means be the more roused to devotion, and better disposed to gather to themselves the fruits of grace which come from the celebration of the sacred mysteries.

TLS yokes the purpose of worship music with the purpose of the liturgy in general. The liturgy's purpose is declared to be simultaneously God-oriented and humanity-oriented. Any attempt to emphasize one to the exclusion of the other is to misunderstand the liturgy's very nature. Roman Catholic liturgical worship has both anaphoric (lifting up to God) and katabatic (descending toward humanity) dimensions.

On the one hand, God is glorified in the liturgy (and therefore by worship music used in the liturgy). The notion of "glory" is multivalent in both Scripture and tradition. Exegetes inform us that twenty-five different Hebrew terms are translated by the Greek *doxa* in the Septuagint. The most important of the Hebrew terms is *kabod,* which denotes heaviness or weightiness, and thus importance. Within the Hebrew worldview, the glory of God manifests itself whenever God's importance is felt. Natural phenomena such as fire, cloud, thunder, lightning, or storm may all disclose God's glory to the observer, just as historical acts such as the Exodus from Egypt, the forging of the Sinai covenant, or the inspired actions of prophets may reveal it. Human beings glorify God whenever they acknowledge God's importance in natural phenomena and the movements of history. For Christians, in addition to God's self-revelation in nature and history, the glory of God is manifest in God's self-communication in Jesus of Nazareth. His life and deeds, his mission and ministry, his death and destiny reveal God's glory in human form. Christians glorify God when they faithfully acknowledge what God is and does, when they recognize and celebrate what God has done and is doing through Christ in the power of the Spirit (creating, redeeming, and sustaining space, time, matter, and spirit), when they commit themselves and proclaim to others God's true weight in the scheme of things.

On the other hand, liturgy (and therefore worship music used in the liturgy) transforms the participants in holiness and builds them up in faith. Like the concept of glory, sanctification and edification are polysemous in both Scripture and tradition. At its core sanctification means the condition or process by which human beings participate in the very holiness of God. In Eastern traditions, the process of entering into this life of holiness is frequently called *theopoiēsis* (deification), with the emphasis placed on the divine philanthropy bending down to reconstitute and transform human beings by the power of the Holy Spirit. In Western traditions, this process was often conceptualized as *dikaiosunē* (justification), with the stress placed on God's gracious acts in forgiving sinners, reconciling and reincorporating those who were estranged from friendship with God and neighbor. In both, however, the liturgy is identified as the preeminent place for God's activity in bringing human beings into union with God, where forgiven sinners become radiant with God's own life. Edification, probably related to the Pauline term *oikodomē,* has at its root the notion of (re)constructing a house, building, or temple and is used metaphorically to refer to the building up and strengthening of the Church. (It is possible that the term is omitted when TLS is quoted in later documents because of the negative connotations and class overtones that the term had acquired in vernacular languages.) Thus the fundamental purpose of worship music in Roman Rite liturgy is to transform human beings in grace as, Spirit-filled, they acknowledge God's deeds, preeminently in Jesus.

TLS then sketches two functions for worship music that would help to fulfill its purpose in liturgy. The first function, corresponding to glorifying God, is adding ceremonial splendor to the enacted rites. In a certain sense the beauty of liturgical worship becomes a sublime expression of the truth of the religious experience it enshrines and the religious vision it proclaims.[1] Far from finding its parallels in the use of music to signal the importance of monarchs or presidents, worship music used ceremonially does not call attention to the human actors in the liturgy, but to God encountering God's people in the liturgical transaction.

The second function, corresponding to sanctifying and edifying the faithful, is heightening the effectiveness of the texts proclaimed. Somewhat surprisingly, the document declares that the liturgical texts are proposed "for the understanding of the faithful," although they remain in Latin, Greek, and Hebrew. Music conjoined with certain of these texts is to provide a subtle kind of commentary, a first interpretation of the biblical and liturgical texts by emphasizing certain words or syllables through particular musical modes, elongations, pitches, phrases, etc. While the musical-textual complex may have psychological and emotional consequences, its primary function is to stimulate the worshipers' will: texted worship music, whether listened to or personally performed, should lead worshipers to a whole-hearted commitment to God in Christ. The use of the term "efficacious" and the phrase "better disposed to gather to themselves the fruits of grace" reminds one of scholastic theories of sacramental causality in which sacramental celebration caused grace *ex opere operato* in the recipient who did not place an *obex* (obstacle) to the sacrament's activity; when the *obex* was removed the fruits of the sacrament could be enjoyed. Analogously, chanted liturgical texts may cause a transformation in holiness in the worshiper who allows these texts to be more than purely informational.

Note that TLS emphasizes the logocentric (word-oriented) character of worship music without providing a theoretical justification for nontexted music in Roman Rite worship. There is nothing in TLS 1 to support the use of purely instrumental music to create a mood or emotional aura during liturgy.

Musicae sacrae disciplina

MSD positions its discussion of the purpose of worship music in the context of a general theory of art:

24. The ordination and direction of man to his ultimate end—which is God—by absolute and necessary law based on the nature and infinite perfection of God Himself is so solid that not even God could exempt anyone from it. . . . Since man is born to attain this supreme end, he ought to conform himself and through his actions direct all the powers of his body and his soul, rightly ordered among themselves and duly subjected to the end they are meant to attain, to the divine Model. Therefore even art and works of art must be judged in the light of their conformity and concord with man's last end.

25. Art certainly must be listed among the noblest manifestations of human genius. Its purpose is to express in human works the infinite beauty of which it is, as it were, the reflection. . . .

27. Since this is true of works of art in general, it obviously applies also to religious and sacred art. Actually religious art is even more closely bound to God and the promotion of His praise and glory, because its only purpose is to give the faithful the greatest aid in turning their minds piously to God through the works it directs to their senses of sight and hearing.

MSD yokes the meaning of art to the meaning of human life in general. It asserts that human life has a purpose (in contrast to those thinkers who hold that human life is meaningless or absurd), that that purpose is not self-generated (in contrast to certain atheistic or agnostic existentialists or ethical egoists), and that that purpose is not constructed by sub- or transhuman forces (in contrast to types of Marxism, naturalism, psychologism, etc.). It affirms that God has created human beings for a definite purpose: free and complete loving union with God. Producing and engaging works of art either promotes or discourages loving union with God. Art must then be judged not for its own sake, as a pleasure-inducing decorative accretion, as an expression of the artist's psyche, or as an embodiment of the "spirit of an age," but insofar as it reveals God's will for humanity and supports and sustains humanity's quest for union with God. Religious art shares in the *telos* of all art but brings to explicit attention the beauty, goodness, and truth of God as humanity's ultimate end.

On this basis MSD argues that music occupies a special category among religious arts:

30. These laws and standards for religious art apply in a stricter and holier way to sacred music because sacred music enters more intimately into divine worship than many other liberal arts, such as architecture, painting and sculpture. These last serve to prepare a worthy setting for the sacred ceremonies. Sacred music, however, has an important place in the actual performance of the sacred ceremonies and rites themselves. Hence the Church must take the greatest care to prevent whatever might be unbecoming to sacred worship or anything that might distract the

faithful in attendance from lifting their minds up to God from entering into sacred music, which is the servant, as it were, of the sacred liturgy.

31. The dignity and lofty purpose of sacred music consists in the fact that its lovely melodies and splendor beautify and embellish the voices of the priest who offers Mass and of the Christian people who praise the Sovereign God. . . .

34. It is easy to infer from what has just been said that the dignity and force of sacred music are greater the closer sacred music itself approaches to the supreme act of Christian worship, the Eucharistic sacrifice of the altar. . . .

35. To this highest function of sacred music we must add another which closely resembles it, that is, its function of accompanying and beautifying other liturgical ceremonies, particularly the recitation of the Divine Office in choir.

Like TLS, MSD emphasizes texted worship music as normative in the Roman Rite, although it recognizes the role purely instrumental music may play in the liturgy. The special position texted worship music has among the arts employed in worship arises from the fact that, in certain cases, it is by means of music that the rite is accomplished. The priest who chants a preface, the cantor who intones a litany, the schola that vocalizes the Gloria, and the assembly that sings the Sanctus-Benedictus are all transacting liturgical events by means of music.

Echoing TLS's teaching, MSD indicates two primary functions for worship music employed in the liturgy: the glorification of God and the sanctification and edification of the faithful:

31. . . . . [Sacred music's] special power and excellence should lift up to God the minds of the faithful who are present. It should make the liturgical prayers of the Christian community more alive and fervent so that everyone can praise and beseech the Triune God more powerfully, more intently, and more effectively. . . .

32. The power of sacred music increases the honor given to God by the Church in union with Christ, its Head. Sacred music likewise helps to increase the fruits which the faithful, moved by the sacred harmonies, derive from the holy liturgy. These fruits, as daily experience and many ancient and modern literary sources show, manifest themselves in a life and conduct worthy of a Christian.

MSD adduces an additional function for music—educational or catechetical inculcation of religious doctrine—but associates this function not with sacred, but with religious music:

36. We must also hold in honor that music which is not primarily a part of the sacred liturgy, but which by its power and purpose greatly aids re-

ligion. . . . As experience shows, it can exercise great and salutary force
and power on the souls of the faithful, both when it is used in churches
during non-liturgical services and ceremonies, or when it is used outside
churches at various solemnities and celebrations.

37. The tunes of these hymns, which are often sung in the language of the
people, are memorized with almost no effort or labor. The mind grasps
the words and the music. They are frequently repeated and completely
understood. Hence even boys and girls, learning these sacred hymns at a
tender age, are greatly helped by them to know, appreciate and memorize
the truths of the faith. Therefore they also serve as a sort of catechism.

The 1958 Instruction

In presenting its justification for the various detailed guidelines it
presents, 1958Inst confirms the purpose of worship music employed in
the liturgy as presented in TLS and MSD:

23. It is necessary . . . to regulate the various means by which the faithful can actively participate in the most holy Sacrifice of the Mass so as to
remove danger of any abuse and to achieve the chief purpose of this participation, which is a more complete worship of God and the edification
of the faithful.

What is new in the document is its attempt to categorize the various forms of liturgical participation. We have already seen that MSD
distinguishes between direct and indirect liturgical participation. If, as
TLS and MSD assert, human beings are transformed in holiness by par-
ticipating in the liturgy, the modes of such engagement are multiple:

22. Of its nature the Mass demands that all those who are present should
participate, each in his own proper way.

a. This participation must first of all be *interior,* exercised in the pious attention of the soul and in the affections of the heart. Through this, the
faithful "closely join the Supreme Priest and together with Him and
through Him offer the Sacrifice and consecrate themselves together with
Him.". . .

b. The participation of those present is more complete if this interior attention is joined to an *exterior* participation manifested by external acts,
such as the position of the body (kneeling, standing, sitting), ritual gestures, and, above all, by the responses, prayers and chants. . . .

c. Finally, perfect active participation is achieved when there is also *sacramental* participation, by which the "faithful who are present communicate
not only with spiritual affection, but also in reception of the Sacrament of
the Eucharist, so that they derive greater fruit from this most blessed
Sacrifice."

While worship music cannot bring about a properly sacramental participation (which would involve direct reception of a sacrament, such as consuming the consecrated bread and/or wine at Eucharist, being anointed with oil of the sick in Extreme Unction, etc.), it can promote both interior and exterior participation in worshipers. Those who listen attentively to worship music being sung or played during liturgy, and by means of this attentive listening allow their spirits to conjoin with the offering of Christ and the Church, cultivate interior participation. But such interior participation can also be expressed and deepened when worshipers directly produce worship music during liturgy in responses, prayers, and chants. 1958Inst is careful not to play interior participation off against exterior participation, although listing interior participation first should caution worshipers against worship music that only produces feelings of togetherness, psychological release, or aesthetic delight without a direct referent to the Transcendent.

Sacrosanctum Concilium

SC quotes TLS when presenting its own teaching about the purpose of worship music employed in liturgy. Perhaps significantly, it omits the phrase "and edification" (of the faithful) in delineating this purpose:

> 112. . . . The Council, keeping the norms and precepts of ecclesiastical tradition and discipline and having regard to the purpose of sacred music, which is the glory of God and the sanctification of the faithful, decrees what follows.

A new nuance in magisterial teaching on Roman Rite worship music appears when the same article refers to the *munus ministeriale* of worship music:

> 112. Holy Scripture itself has bestowed praise upon sacred song and the same may be said of the Fathers of the Church and of the Roman pontiffs, who in recent times . . . have explained more precisely the ministerial function supplied by sacred music in the service of the Lord.

Lucien Deiss, in discussing the meaning of *munus ministeriale* applied to Roman Rite worship music, claims that it can be defined only in reference to the liturgy itself as understood and interpreted by authority and in reference to the very congregation involved in the celebration, ultimately, to the people of God celebrating Jesus Christ:

> The expression "ministerial function" is a literal but useful translation of the Latin *munus minsteriale*. The word *munus* denotes duty or function;

the adjective *ministeriale* (which has the same root as *munus*) evokes a similar idea of service. In the liturgy, the *munus ministeriale* or the ministerial function of a person or thing is the particular service given to the community in celebration of the liturgy. . . . Liturgical song fulfills its ministerial function by *performing a service* to the liturgy, on the one hand, and to the community celebrating it, on the other.[2]

SC 112 lists three functions for worship music as it attempts to achieve its *munus ministeriale:*

> 112. . . . Therefore sacred music will be the more holy the more closely it is joined to the liturgical rite, whether by adding delight to prayer, fostering oneness of spirit, or investing the rites with greater solemnity.

"Investing the rites with greater solemnity" *(ritus sacros maiore locupletans sollemnitate)* recalls the ceremonial function of worship music associated with divine glorification in TLS. But the other two functions are new articulations of the task of worship music to transform worshipers in holiness. "Adding delight to prayer" is not to be interpreted as providing psychological or emotional uplift by means of entertaining sounds, making the bitter medicine of prayer more palatable through a sugary spoonful of music. The Latin phrase *orationem suavius exprimens* might be more literally translated "expressing prayer more pleasantly"; the emphasis remains on interior and exterior participation in the liturgical act, engaged in a more gratifying way through worship music. "Fostering oneness of spirit" *(fovens unanimitatem)* is likewise to be understood as something more than engendering superficial and passing fellow-feeling. Liturgical unity is not founded on kinship ties, ethnic heritage, economic parity, shared ideology, or common emotion (although all of these may be manifest in a unified liturgical assembly). Rather, liturgical unity stems from the action of God through Christ in the Holy Spirit calling people out to be the Church of God *(ekklēsia tou theou)*. Worship music employed in the liturgy may help to express and deepen this spiritual union.

Musicam Sacram

It should not be surprising that MS quotes TLS (in the form modified by SC) to define the purpose of worship music employed in Roman Rite liturgy:

> 4. The reasonable expectation is that in welcoming and carrying out these norms, pastors, composers, and the faithful, will strive with one accord to achieve the genuine purpose of sacred music, "which is the glory of God and the sanctification of the faithful."

However, MS provides a new five-fold taxonomy of the functions worship music provides in achieving this purpose:

> 5. A liturgical service takes on a nobler aspect when the rites are cele-brated with singing, the ministers of each rank take their parts in them, and the congregation actively participates. This form of celebration gives a more graceful expression to prayer and brings out more distinctly the hierarchic character of the liturgy and the specific make-up of the com-munity. It achieves a closer union of hearts through the union of voices. It raises the mind more readily to heavenly realities through the splendor of the rites. It makes the whole celebration a more striking symbol of the celebration to come in the heavenly Jerusalem.

First, MS lists an alluring or decorative function for worship music when it asserts that singing "gives a more graceful expression to prayer." The document recognizes that music has sensual appeal, that it can influence psychological states, that it can clothe language in such a way that the sentiments expressed gain more powerful emotional resonances. But MS does not limit worship music to a decorative func-tion, understanding music simply as an aesthetic enrichment of litur-gical rite, a potentially pleasant but by no means necessary addition to the prescribed texts and ceremonies. While worship music may be al-luring, it must also provide other functions.

Second, MS registers a differentiating function, noting that singing "brings out more distinctly the hierarchic character of the liturgy and the specific make-up of the community." What texts are sung when and by whom discloses liturgical roles operating within the ecclesiastical community. MS 6 further specifies this function:

> To give its true structure to the celebration of the liturgy requires, first, the proper assignment of functions and the kind of execution in which "each one, minister or layperson, who has an office to perform, does all of, but only, those parts which pertain to that office by the nature of the rite and the principles of liturgy." But an additional requirement is exact fidelity to the meaning and character of each part and of each song. To achieve this end it is above all necessary that those parts which of their nature call for singing are in fact sung and in the style and form demanded by the parts themselves.

Notice that this differentiating function operates both personally and structurally. Certain chants are reserved to ordained ministers (e.g., "The Lord be with you" dialogue), other chants may be led by a can-tor (e.g., the litany of the saints at an ordination), others may be exe-cuted by a choir/schola (e.g., the Glory to God), while still others are in the purview of the entire assembly (e.g., the Holy, Holy, Holy).

Refusing to respect these personnel distinctions is to distort the liturgical expression of the structuring of the Church. But distortion can also occur when elements intended to be sung are recited or when the genres of the various elements of worship music are not respected. Reciting an entrance antiphon does not respect its function as opening music accompanying the procession of the ministers at the beginning of Mass, and reciting the Glory to God does not conform to the definition in *General Instruction of the Roman Missal*[3] [hereafter GIRM] 31 of this element as a "hymn" (although both practices are presently allowed in the rubrics). The Sanctus, Anamnesis, and Amen of the Eucharistic Prayer are acclamations, the Kyrie Eleison and Agnus Dei are litanies, the Exsultet is a lyric proclamation; musical settings should respect the fundamental structures of these elements.

Third, MS records a unifying function for worship music, reinforcing the unifying function mentioned in SC 112. TLS had claimed that the universal character of Gregorian chant made it eminently suitable for unifying the diverse personalities and groupings that comprise the liturgical assembly. Conciliar and post-conciliar documentation, recognizing the historical, linguistic, and cultural limits of the Gregorian repertoire, no longer makes this claim. But the search for music that genuinely unites believers in heartfelt worship continues, perhaps especially intensely in nations like the United States, Canada, and Australia where Roman Catholic congregations include so many ethnic and linguistic groups.

Fourth, MS specifies a transcendental function for worship music, asserting that it "raises the mind more readily to heavenly realities through the splendor of the rites." A subtle transformation has taken place: where before splendor in ceremonial and the music which accompanied it was yoked to the purpose of glorifying God, it is now associated with transforming the worshipers' attitudes.

Finally, MS notes an eschatological function for worship music, asserting that music "makes the whole celebration a more striking symbol of the celebration to come in the heavenly Jerusalem." Both Jewish and Christian Scriptures image heavenly worship in terms of song performed by the angels, creatures, elders, and saints in concert. A concluding phrase in certain Roman Rite prefaces expresses this eschatological function well: "With angels and archangels, with thrones and dominations, and with the whole band of the heavenly armies, we sing a hymn to the glory of God, chanting without end." Although technically this eschatological function refers to the mirroring of the heavenly liturgy by its earthly participants, there is also a sense in which the use of worship music from other eras connects us with those "who have gone before us in faith" and are now celebrating celestial worship. An exclusive diet of contemporary worship music would defeat this eschatological function.

Music in Catholic Worship

Turning from documents intended for the entire Roman Rite to directives for Roman Rite worshipers in the United States, we see a strong emphasis on and development of the *munus ministeriale* of worship music. MCW interprets the ministerial function of music as follows:

> 23. . . . The function of music is ministerial; it must serve and never dominate. Music should assist the assembled believers to express and share the gift of faith that is within them and to nourish and strengthen their interior commitment of faith. It should heighten the texts so that they speak more fully and more effectively. The quality of joy and enthusiasm which music adds to community worship cannot be gained in any other way. It imparts a sense of unity to the congregation and sets the appropriate tone for a particular celebration.

> 24. In addition to expressing texts, music can also unveil a dimension of meaning and feeling, a communication of ideas and intuitions which words alone cannot yield. This dimension is integral to the human personality and to growth in faith. It cannot be ignored if the signs of worship are to speak to the whole person. . . .

As TLS had taught, worship music is to heighten the effectiveness of the liturgical texts in reinforcing the worshiper's wills in faith but, unlike TLS's teaching, these texts are no longer limited to Latin, Greek, and Hebrew. Like MS, MCW records a unifying function for worship music: by means of shared music making the unity of the liturgical assembly is both expressed and deepened.

But what is most noticeable in comparison to the Roman documents is MCW's attention to the psychological effects and emotional consequences generated by worship music. Perhaps because it rejects a purely notional form of liturgical participation, MCW emphasizes feeling as "integral to the human personality and to growth in faith." Worship music, if it is to speak to the whole person, must manifest its emotional power (although only joy and enthusiasm are recorded among the possible emotions triggered by worship music).

Liturgical Music Today

In contrast to earlier documents' emphasis upon the alluring, differentiating, unifying, transcendental, and eschatological functions of worship music or its psychological and emotional effects, LMT emphasizes its functions within ritual:

> 9. The various functions of sung prayer must be distinguished within liturgical rites. Sometimes song is meant to accompany ritual actions. In such cases the song is not independent but serves, rather, to support the prayer of the assembly when an action requires a longer period of time or when the action is going to be repeated several times. The music enriches the moments and keeps it from becoming burdensome.
>
> 10. At other times in the liturgical action the sung prayer itself is a constituent element of the rite. While it is being prayed, no other ritual action is being performed. . . . In each of these cases the music does not serve as a mere accompaniment, but as the integral mode by which the mystery is proclaimed and presented.

The two fundamental categories thus become music that underscores some other ritual event and music that, in and of itself, constitutes the rite. (It should be clear that this dual categorization is furthered in the four-fold categorization of Edward Foley and Mary McGann mentioned above.)

The Milwaukee Report

Presupposing the assertions made in the earlier documents explored above about the purpose and functions of Roman Rite worship music, MR emphasizes the symbolic function of worship music, situating it as a particular manifestation of the symbolic character of sound itself and of the liturgy:

> 12. A symbol both expresses what we believe and shapes that belief. Although symbols employ the created world, they are themselves actions. The sacraments are ecclesial symbols. . . . We acknowledge that Christ is the primordial sacrament, that the church is the abiding presence of that primordial sacrament in the world and is foundational for all other sacraments. Thus the Second Vatican Council teaches that the church is the sacrament of Christ who, in turn, is the source of every other sacrament.

The assertions in article 12 draw on the work of philosophers such as Suzanne Langer,[4] Ernst Cassirer,[5] and Paul Ricoeur[6] to present symbols as actions rather than things, complex negotiations by which human beings encounter and structure reality. Ideas proposed by theologians such as Otto Semmelroth,[7] Karl Rahner,[8] and Edward Schillebeeckx[9] ground the articles' notions of (the humanity of) Christ as sacrament of God, the Church as sacrament of Christ, and the Church's official communal rituals as its sacraments. It should be clear that these thinkers do not conceptualize a symbol as a pointer to an absent reality, but rather the means by which depth reality manifests its presence to human consciousness *(Realsymbol)*.

Within this philosophical and theological framework, sound itself is explored for its symbolic capacities:

> 13. Music is part of the symbolic language of worship. Music's sacramental power is rooted in the nature of sound, the raw material for music. Sound itself is our starting point for understanding music and its capacity to serve as a vehicle for God's self-revelation. Sound's temporality, for example, symbolizes a God active in creation and history; its seemingly insubstantial nature symbolizes a God who is both present and hidden; its dynamism symbolizes a God who calls us into dialogue; its ability to unify symbolizes our union with God and others; its evocation of personal presence symbolizes a God whom we perceive as personal. So sounds themselves, from a Judaeo-Christian perspective, can be part of the self-revelation of God. Although sound can be destructive and a source of division, our tradition affirms music's capacity to serve as a vehicle of God's self-revelation without localizing or confining God.

Edward Foley expands upon these insights in his essay "Toward a Sound Theology," yoking the five properties of sound listed in MR 13 with their distinct revelation of God as understood in the Judaeo-Christian tradition. First he conjoins the experience of sound as impermanent with the revelation of God as historical:

> Sound events like music or speech are impermanent events which exist for the listener only in the doing of them—only for the duration of the performance. Thus sound events like music are fundamental experiences of change: one note or syllable or lapping wave in sequence after another. . . .
>
> Sound events are time-bound, history-bound events. Because of this existential quality, music is able to image of God who, in the Judaeo-Christian tradition, intervenes in time and reveals Self in human history. Furthermore, this time-bound art has the ability to engage the community in the present reality of worship and signal that union with God is an existential possibility, here and now.[10]

Attending to the difference between music in performance and its encoding by means of a musical score or retrieval mechanism (such as a record, tape, or CD) may offer some interesting parallels to the notion of God's primal revelation in history and that revelation's encoding in oral tradition, written Scriptures, commentaries, etc. Similarly notions of liturgical anamnesis may be clarified with reference to existential quality of music: the liturgy, while shaped over history, does not mime the past but enacts divine encounter in the present, much as contemporary music performances do not reproduce past acoustic events but allow encounter with them in the present.

Second, Foley connects the experience of sound as intangible with the revelation of God as an elusive presence:

> The paradox of all sound phenomena like speech or music is that they are perceivable but elusive, recognizable but uncontainable. . . . This experience of the apparent intangibility of sound phenomenon is heightened by the fact that sound phenomena are perceptible by only one sense. Whereas oil paints, sandstone, and steel can been [sic] seen, touched, and—if one wishes—tasted, sound is usually only heard. Music in particular is not only perceived as insubstantial but itself seems to have an "ambivalence of content.". . .

> The apparently insubstantial nature of music is one of the reasons why it has symbolized the mysterious and wholly other since the dawn of creation. Music, as a nondiscursive symbol, . . . is especially distinguished by its ambivalence of content. . . . In the Judaeo-Christian tradition music is an effective means for communicating with a God who is both present and hidden. Furthermore, music offers itself as a powerful symbol for the divine Self who is recognizable while remaining the unnameable. Music thus enables us to encounter and know God without presuming to capture or contain the divine Self.[11]

Though one might argue that sound phenomena are not only heard but felt (as, for example, in a rock concert), Foley's discussion of the insubstantial character of acoustic phenomena clearly grounds the transcendental and eschatological functions of worship music delineated in MS in the very nature of sound.

Third, Foley couples the experience of music as active with the revelation of God as dynamic:

> Because sound events are fundamentally temporal events and perdure only as long as the sound is being generated, they have an inherent dynamism about them. . . . Sound waves . . . move fast enough to communicate movement yet slow enough to be perceived as moving. . . . Human physiology contributes to the illusion that sound events are dynamic events. The human ear, for example, is able to distinguish two clicks separated by only two or three thousandths of a second, while the human eye can only distinguish the flashing of a light at between a fifteenth and a sixtieth [sic] of a second. Beyond this point the human observer no longer experiences a flashing light but continuous illumination. Humans have more developed physiological capacities for hearing than for seeing. . . .

> Because of sound's ability to resonate inside two individuals at the same time, it has the capacity to strike a common chord and elicit sympathetic

vibrations from those who hear it. It is dynamic in its ability to enter the world of the other and elicit a response. Thus music effectively reflects the dialogic impulse of God in the Judaeo-Christian tradition who continuously initiates dialogue with believers. This characteristic emphasizes not only God's historical intervention or personal nature but further embodies the belief that God has been and continues to be engaged in the individual and corporate life of humankind.[12]

Perhaps the experience of sound as dynamic can be yoked to the differentiating function of worship music articulated in MS: sound as the dynamism by which dialogic interchange can take place differentiates the interlocutors.

Fourth, Foley links the experience of sound as an invitation to engagement with the revelation of God as relational:

Sound events like poetry or music are essentially acts of engagement. . . . Thus some have suggested that sound events like human song are fundamentally unitive: uniting singer with the song, listener with the song, singer with the listener, the listener with other listeners, and even in a new way the listener with her or himself. To be in the presence of a sound event is to be engaged in that sound event and to be engaged with both the producer of the sound and with the others who hear it. . . . Thus the ear is the metaphor for human beings born open to engagement, not just with sounds, but with the people who produce them. Consequently the ear could be considered a physiological metaphor for relationship. . . .

Closely related to the dynamic character of the Judaeo-Christian God is the relational basis of this revelation. The God of Jews and Christians not only reveals Self in time—in a dynamic way that calls forth an individual response from believers—but is a God who also calls us into relationship with Godself and each other. . . . Ultimately, the God of Judaeo-Christian revelation is one who calls forth a network of relationships, sealed in a covenant. . . . Sound events such as music, therefore, are strong metaphors for the God who calls us and for the network of relationships demanded by such a call.[13]

Thus the declarations of SC, MS, and MCW that worship music can have a unifying function are grounded in the very nature of sound and deepened to include multiple forms of unity.

Finally, Foley associates the experience of sound as personal to the revelation of God as personal:

Sound events . . . are not simply experiences of something other, but of *an*other. Sound encounters are keyed to be personal encounters. . . . Acoustic space does not, like visual space, contain a thing, but is a sphere delineated by activity. And such acoustic activity is translated by the human imagination as evidence of animation, of life, and particularly of human presence. . . . It is in the acoustic arena that Martin Buber's relational paradigm of the "I-Thou" becomes fully possible. . . .

Not only is the God of Judaeo-Christian revelation recognized as a power intervening in history and calling us into relationship, but more so is this God imaged as a person who intervenes on behalf of a beloved. . . . Not an impersonal natural power or some arbitrary force of fate, this is a personal God who loves. . . . The sound event by its very nature supports the revelation of a God who is perceived as a person. Music, in particular, is an infallible indicator of human presence, since music, properly speaking, is a human creation that does not otherwise occur in nature. Consequently, music serves as a special sound metaphor for the unnameable God who chooses to reveal Self in personal terms.[14]

If, as MR asserts and Foley explicates, sound itself is symbolic, music as a particular manifestation of sound is likewise symbolic:

14. Music, as the most refined of all sound phenomena, does even more to serve as a vehicle for God's self-revelation. For example, rhythmic elements underscore the temporality of human existence into which God has intervened, and a familiar melody can contribute to a heightened experience of unity with each other and God. In Christianity, music becomes one with the liturgy, which is the church's first theology and the primary expression of the church's belief. Because sound and, by extension, music are natural vehicles for the self-revelation of the God of Judaeo-Christian revelation, and because liturgy is the locus for encounter with and the revelation of such a God, it is understandable why music unites itself so intimately to Christian liturgy. The combination of the two enables the possibility of encounter and revelation as no other combination of human artifacts and faith event.

15. Music's power in ritual can be further understood by reflecting on the word-centered nature of Judaeo-Christian revelation and liturgy. The God of Abraham and of Jesus is not only perceived as a personal God but also as the God who speaks and whose word is both law and life. God's word is at the core of Judaeo-Christian revelation and worship. Just as the inflection of human speech shapes the meaning of our words, so can music open up new meanings in sung texts as well as the liturgical unit that is the setting for such texts. Furthermore, the extended duration that musical performance adds to a text, which usually takes more time to sing than to speak, can contribute to the heightening and opening up of a text.

The natural alliance between text and tune is at the heart of the relationship between music and Christian liturgy. Music, like no other art form, has a special capacity to heighten and serve the word that occupies a central place in worship. Such an awareness was reflected in SC: When noting the integral relationship between music and liturgy, the bishops pointed in particular to the binding of sacred song and text as the main reason for this integrity.

> 16. Music has a natural capacity to unite the singer with the song, the singer with those who listen, singers with each other. Christian ritual song joins the assembly with Christ, who is the source and the content of the song. The song of the assembly is an event of the presence of Christ. What fuller assertion could there be of the sacramental nature of Christian ritual music, especially the song of the assembly? Sacramental language should be employed for Christian ritual music because, more than any other language available to us, it effectively underscores and communicates music's power in worship.

With these three articles themes we have noted in earlier documents reappear in a new guise. MR 14 gives theoretical grounding to the use of both texted and nontexted music in liturgy, while reasserting music's preeminent role among the arts employed in worship. MR 15 acknowledges the privileged position texted music holds in Roman Rite worship and provides an extended gloss on TLS's assertion that the chief duty of worship music is to clothe the liturgical text with such suitable melody that it becomes efficacious in the spiritual lives of worshipers. MR 16 reaffirms the unifying function of worship music but makes the daring claim that Christ is the source and content of Christian ritual song, one of the means by which the risen Lord is made effectively present to the praying Church.

The Snowbird Statement

Like MR, SS presupposes the assertions made in earlier documents about the purpose and functions of Roman Catholic worship music. But where MR concentrates on the symbolic functions of worship music, SS explores its aesthetic character:

> 3. We believe that beauty is essential in the liturgical life and mission of the church. Beauty is an effective—even sacramental—sign of God's presence and action in the world. The beautiful expresses the joy and delight which prefigure the glory of the liturgy of the heavenly Jerusalem. An injustice is committed against God's people when styles of worship and liturgical art are promoted which lack aesthetic beauty. The problem is evidenced when the church's worship becomes committed to pragmatic, ideological or political ends. Even a liturgy which serves the truth of faith and the justice of the Gospel is insufficient when the beauty of God's self-revelation is inadequately expressed and celebrated. While not wishing to promote aestheticism, we encourage a new attention to the theology and practice of beauty in Catholic worship, especially in the area of litur-

gical music. This will necessitate a more intense and sustained engagement with theological and philosophical aesthetics.

Whereas Roman Catholic theology has strongly developed approaches to the mystery of God in terms of being (the metaphysics of presence), truth (the intelligibility of the divine), and goodness (the moral order), approaches to the mystery of God in terms of beauty (a theological aesthetics) have been comparatively underdeveloped. This deficiency has had an impact on Roman Catholic worship life and may be remedied by attention to the theological aesthetics developed by Eastern theologians and contemporary thinkers such as Hans Urs von Balthasar and Aidan Nichols.[15]

The following chapter will explore the qualities worship music must have if it is to give glory to God and sanctify the faithful by making prayer more alluring and memorable, by differentiating ritual roles, by unifying worshipers, by calling attention to transcendental realities, and by evoking heavenly worship in the symbolic and beautiful interactions of Roman Rite liturgy.

ENDNOTES

[1] Robert Taft illustrates the power of beauty in liturgical worship as reflective of religious truth as he recounts the legendary origins of Christianity in Kiev: "According to the so-called *Chronicle of Nestor* for the year 987, the Bulgars (Moslems), Germans (Latins), Jews and Greeks had all tried to persuade Prince Vladimir of Kiev to adopt their faith as the religion of Rus. When the prince summoned the notables of the realm to hear their counsel, they advised him: [']You know, oh Prince, that no man condemns his own possessions, but praises them instead. If you desire to make certain, you have servants at your disposal. Send them to inquire about the ritual of each and how he worships God.['] . . .

"Vladimir took their advice and sent out emissaries. When they arrived home, the ambassadors reported to Vladimir. The worship of the Moslems had not impressed them. As for the Germans, they had seen them ['] . . . performing many ceremonies in their temples; but we behold no glory there. Then we went to Greece, and the Greeks led us to the edifices where they worship their God, and we knew not whether we were in heaven or on earth. For on earth there is no such splendor or such beauty, and we are at a loss how to describe it. We only know that God dwells here among men, and their service is fairer than the ceremonies of other nations. For we cannot forget that beauty.'" Robert Taft, "The Spirit of Eastern Christian Worship," *Beyond East and West: Problems in Liturgical Understanding*, NPM Studies in Church Music and Liturgy (Washington, D.C.: The Pastoral Press, 1984) 111–2.

[2] Lucien Deiss, *Spirit and Song of the New Liturgy*, trans. L. L. Haggard and M. L. Mazzarese (Cincinnati: World Library of Sacred Music, 1970) 2, 11. The

author updates his treatment of this topic in *Visions of Liturgy and Music for a New Century,* trans. Jane M.-A. Burton, ed. Donald Molloy (Collegeville: The Liturgical Press, 1996).

[3] The Latin text of the fourth edition of the GIRM appears as "Institutio Generalis Missalis Romani," *Missale Romanum ex decreto Sacrosancti Oecumenici Concilii Vaticani II instauratum auctoritate Pauli Pp. VI promulgatum. Editio typica altera* (Città del Vaticano: Libreria Editrice Vaticana, 1975) 19–92. An English translation appears in DOL nos. 1376–731, pp. 465–533.

[4] Suzanne Langer, *Feeling and Form: A Theory of Art* (New York: Charles Scribner's Sons, 1953); idem, *Philosophy in a New Key: A Study in the Symbolism of Reason, Rite, and Art* (Cambridge, Mass.: Harvard University Press, 1978); idem, *Problems of Art: Ten Philosophical Lectures* (New York: Charles Scribner's Sons, 1957).

[5] Ernst Cassirer, *An Essay on Man* (New Haven, Conn.: Yale University Press, 1955); idem, *The Philosophy of Symbolic Forms,* 3 vols. (New Haven, Conn.: Yale University Press, 1953/1955/1957).

[6] Paul Ricoeur, *The Conflict of Interpretations: Essays in Hermeneutics,* trans. Don Ihde (Evanston, Ill.: Northwestern University Press, 1974); idem, *Interpretation Theory: Discourse and the Surplus of Meaning* (Fort Worth: Texas Christian University Press, 1976); idem, *The Symbolism of Evil,* trans. Emerson Buchanan (Boston: Beacon Press, 1967).

[7] Otto Semmelroth, *Church and Sacrament,* trans. Emily Schossberger (Notre Dame, Ind.: Fides Publishers, 1963).

[8] Karl Rahner, "The Theology of the Symbol," *Theological Investigations IV* (New York: Seabury Press, 1964) 221–52.

[9] Edward Schillebeeckx, *Christ the Sacrament of the Encounter with God,* trans. Cornelius Ernst (Kansas City, Mo.: Sheed Andrews and McMeel, 1963); *Understanding the Faith: Interpretation and Criticism,* trans. N. D. Smith (New York: Seabury Press, 1974).

[10] Edward Foley, "Toward a Sound Theology," *Studia Liturgica* 23 (1993) 124–5, 133.

[11] Ibid., 125, 133.

[12] Ibid., 126, 134.

[13] Ibid., 126–7, 134–5.

[14] Ibid., 127–8, 135.

[15] Initial sources to be consulted include: Paul Evdomikov, *The Art of the Icon: A Theology of Beauty,* trans. Stephen Bigham (Redondo Beach, Calif.: Oakwood Publications, 1990); John Navone, *Toward a Theology of Beauty* (Collegeville: The Liturgical Press, 1996); Aidan Nichols, *The Art of God Incarnate* (London: Darton, Longman and Todd, 1980); Hans Urs von Balthasar, *The Glory of the Lord: A Theological Aesthetics. Volume One: Seeing the Form* (San Francisco: Ignatius Press, 1982).

3

What Qualities Should Roman Catholic Worship Music Exhibit?

The documents under investigation present different understand-ings of what Roman Catholic worship music is with concomitant vari-ety in terminology and the criteria employed to determine its proper language and style. While the documents agree that the purpose of worship music is to glorify God and sanctify the faithful, they vary in their understandings of how worship music functions to fulfill this purpose. In this chapter we will see similar variety in the qualities deemed necessary in Roman Catholic worship music.

Tra le sollecitudini

Just as it grounds the discussion of the definition and purpose of Roman Rite worship music in the twentieth century, so TLS sets the framework for articulating the qualities this music must exhibit:

> 2. Sacred music must . . . eminently possess the qualities which belong to liturgical rites, especially holiness and beauty, from which its other characteristic, universality, will follow spontaneously. It must be holy, and therefore avoid everything that is secular, both in itself and in the way in which it is performed. It must really be an art, since in no other way can it have on the mind of those who hear it that effect which the Church desires in using in her liturgy the art of sound. But it must also be universal in this sense, namely, that although each country may use in its ecclesiastical music whatever special forms may belong to its own na-tional style, these forms must be subject to the proper nature of sacred music, so that it may never produce a bad impression on the mind of any stranger who may hear it.

TLS demands holiness, beauty, and universality as the three qualities to be exhibited by all Roman Catholic worship music. Interestingly, the first two qualities are associated primarily with the liturgical texts and ceremonies that music clothes; music becomes holy and beautiful insofar as it participates in the holiness and beauty of Roman Catholic ritual texts and ceremonies.

TLS presents holiness not with reference to biblical or phenomenological categories *(kabod/doxa, mysterium tremendum et fascinans)*, but as the antithesis of the secular. Not only are holy and secular performance practices distinguishable, TLS claims that holy and secular music can be identified *in se.* As we have noted above, ethnomusicological studies would challenge this categorization. While some cultures clearly distinguish holy from secular music, instruments, performers, or styles, others do not. At particular points in Western European musical tradition, one would be hard pressed to distinguish holy and secular compositions on the basis of instrumentation and style (compare renaissance madrigals and motets or the theatrical and liturgical compositions of Mozart). It is therefore difficult to assign holiness as a quality to music considered in itself without reference to those who employ the music, the texts being sung, the occasions of performance, and the cultural codes by which these elements are organized and to which they contribute.

In TLS the quality of beauty is associated with music's character as true art. It is possible that TLS's defense of sacred music (including chant and classical polyphony) as true art challenges a position in musical aesthetics that connects artistry with an evolutionary perspective. This evolutionary perspective would present artistic progress as movement from simplicity to complexity: from monody through organum and polyphony to melody-with-accompaniment, from modes through major and minor keys to chromaticism, from art as communal expression through art in service to religion to art for art's sake. From this perspective Gregorian chant and classical polyphony would represent archaic and primitive way stations in the evolution of music rather than genuine art. In contrast TLS presents modal monody and polyphony prescribed by liturgical texts as genuine art since beauty can be found in both.

TLS presents universality in Roman Rite worship music with reference to the impression it makes on strangers. It is unclear from the text whether strangers are members of the Roman Rite worshiping outside of their own home culture, Catholics of other rites, non-Roman Catholic Christians, or non-Christians. In any case, according to TLS, universality in Roman Rite worship music arises from its inoffensiveness: no stranger will be scandalized by the music heard during the course of worship.

Musicae sacrae disciplina

MSD affirms the three qualities advanced by TLS while nuancing each of them:

> 42. [Sacred music] must be *holy*. It must not allow within itself anything that savors of the profane nor allow any such thing to slip into the melodies in which it is expressed. The Gregorian chant which has been used in the Church over the course of so many centuries, and which may be called, as it were, its patrimony, is gloriously outstanding for this holiness.

MSD categorizes the holy in opposition to the profane rather than to the secular, but the underlying meaning of the categorization remains the same as in TLS. However, no mention is made of holiness in performance practices, only as a quality that inheres in music *in se,* a quality eminently demonstrated in Gregorian chant. There may be a veiled polemic against worship music that incorporates "profane" melodies (as in the Renaissance practice of using "L'homme armé" as a thematic element in a Mass-setting or the Romantic practice of setting liturgical texts to operatic tunes).

MSD continues TLS's defense of sacred music as genuine art. Instead of a protest against an evolutionary perspective in judging artistic merit, however, MSD notes four factors manifested by chant that establish its claim as genuine art:

> 43. This chant, because of the close adaptation of the melody to the sacred text, is not only most intimately conformed to the words, but also in a way interprets their force and efficacy and brings delight to the minds of the hearers. It does this by the use of musical modes that are simple and plain, but which are still composed with such sublime and holy art that they move everyone to sincere admiration and constitute an almost inexhaustible source from which musicians and composers draw new melody.

First, MSD notes that chant interprets the sacred texts in a nondiscursive way that allows them greater communicative power. Although chant melodies rarely indulge in "tone-painting," the attempt to illustrate notions by melodic curve (e.g., a flurry of notes applied to the word "running"), harmonic language (e.g., minor key for texts about the crucifixion and major key for texts about the resurrection), or recurring sound patterns (e.g., the Wagnerian notion of a *leitmotif* tagging a particular object, person, quality, etc.), some subtle illustrations of the texts are present, though these illustrations seem subordinated to the functions the chants must perform liturgically.

Second, MSD states that chant provides delight to the minds of the hearers. Those who actively engage in performing the chant may react pleasurably to the subtlety of the chant melodies, the discipline of common music making, even to the physiological benefits of breath control developed by chanting. Those who listen may be enchanted by the interplay of text and music, by the religious seriousness of its artistic expression, and/or by a sense of solidarity with other humans who have worshiped using this music in other cultures and times. While chant is never performed solely for aesthetic enjoyment during worship, there is no principle declaring that Catholic worship must be a grim, dour, and humanly unappealing experience.

Third, MSD claims that modal monody, far from being an archaic and primitive instance of musical art, is a system of musical expression eliciting universal admiration. The theoretical underpinnings of chant composition are still being investigated by musical scholars, but all agree that these compositions are not purely spontaneous efflorescences but disciplined combinations of fixed traditional materials with inspired novelty.

Finally, MSD asserts that later composers have found in chant melodies the sources of further artistic creativity, not only in providing instrumental accompaniments for their performance, but in employing them in sacred (e.g., Maurice Duruflé's setting of the "Ubi Caritas" chant) or secular (e.g., Berlioz's or Rachmaninoff's use of the "Dies irae" chant in the *Symphonie Fantastique* and the *Variations on a Theme of Paganini*) compositions.

MSD presents a different understanding of universality than that espoused by TLS:

> 45. The requirements of the other property of sacred music—that property by virtue of which it should be an example of true art—will be duly satisfied. And if in Catholic churches throughout the entire world Gregorian chant sounds forth without corruption or diminution, the chant itself, like the sacred Roman liturgy, will have a characteristic of universality, so that the faithful, wherever they may be, will hear music that is familiar to them and a part of their own home. In this way they may experience, with much spiritual consolation, the wonderful unity of the Church. This is one of the most important reasons why the Church so greatly desires that the Gregorian chant traditionally associated with the Latin words of the sacred liturgy be used.

Where TLS considered the universality of Roman Rite worship music to reside in its inoffensiveness to strangers, MSD associates universality with group identity. The claim is made that a common worship music repertoire experienced by Roman Rite Catholics in different nations and cultures will give them a sense of the transnational and transcultural character of the Church. MSD does not claim that there is a universal impetus among humans to associate their encounter with the divine with music making. Rather it simply notes that a common worship music repertoire will help Roman Rite Catholics "feel at home" wherever they may be worshiping.

Musicam Sacram

Neither 1958Inst nor SC discusses the qualities deemed necessary for Roman Rite worship music, but MS breaks new ground on this topic. Although it does not deny that holiness, beauty, and universality are appropriate qualities for Roman Rite worship music, the document proffers more functional categories:

> 9. The choice of the style of music for a choir or congregation should be guided by the abilities of those who must do the singing. The Church does not exclude any type of sacred music from liturgical services so long as the music matches the spirit of the service itself and the character of the individual parts and is not a hindrance to the required active participation of the people.

> 10. It is advisable that there be as much suitable variety as possible in the forms of celebration and the degree of participation in proportion to the solemnity of the day and of the assembly, in order that the faithful will more willingly and effectively contribute their own participation.

> 11. The real solemnity of a liturgical service . . . depends not on a more ornate musical style or more ceremonial splendor but on a worthy and reverent celebration. This means respect for the integrity of the rites, that is, carrying out each of the parts in keeping with its proper character. More ornate styles of singing and greater ceremonial splendor are obviously sometimes desirable, when they are possible. But it would be in conflict with the genuine solemnity of a liturgical service if such things were to cause any element of the service to be omitted, altered, or performed improperly.

In these articles MS articulates five qualities necessary in Roman Catholic worship music in addition to holiness, beauty, and universality, qualities formulated by positive and negative criteria. First, Roman Catholic worship music must "match the spirit of the liturgical service"; presumably the converse is reprobated. (As was noted above, cultural codes will have great impact upon determining which music conforms to the liturgy's spirit.) Second, Roman Catholic worship music must fulfill the ritual requirements of the individual elements of the liturgy; conversely, music that hinders or voids the ritual function of individual elements of the liturgy must not be employed. (Thus, e.g., a musical setting of the Creed in which the assembly has no vocal role would be inappropriate.) Third, Roman Catholic worship music must be within the capabilities of the actual worshiping assembly; conversely, music that "hinders the rightful participation of the faithful" must be eliminated. (This does not eliminate more complex music sung and played by musical professionals; it simply declares that such music making may not substitute for the assembly's song at particular points of the liturgy.) Fourth, Roman Catholic worship music must exhibit variety, both in the forms of celebration and in the degree of participation; conversely, a monotonous musical repertoire cannot be sustained. (For example, eucharistic celebrations are no longer designated as *missa lecta* or *missa cantata*; the amount and style of music making at a given liturgy demands pastoral creativity rather than simply conformity to rubrical prescriptions.) Finally, Roman Catholic worship music must respect the character of festivity, both objective (as given in the Roman Calendar) and subjective (as experienced in the make-up of the concrete worshiping assembly).

Thus in addition to holiness, beauty, and universality, Roman Catholic worship music must exhibit spiritual affinity with the liturgy, ritual appropriateness, the capacity to be performed by the assembled worshipers, intelligent variety, and suitable festivity.

Music in Catholic Worship

Commentators agree that the foremost contribution MCW makes to post-Vatican II worship music renewal is its call for a threefold judgment to be made on every musical element employed in Roman Rite worship. It should be clear that the conceptualization of this threefold judgment applies the assertions of MS to the United States scene:

> 25. To determine the value of a given musical element in a liturgical celebration a threefold judgment must be made: musical, liturgical, and pastoral.

Although later articles in MCW seem to treat this single tripartite judgment as three separate (and hierarchically gradated) determinations, article 25 demands that every musical piece employed in Roman Rite worship exhibit three qualities: it must be musically good, liturgically appropriate, and pastorally sound. Having offered this framework, the document provides further specifications of each of the qualities demanded.

MCW begins its explication of the musical dimension needed in Roman Rite worship music with a strong call for artistic excellence:

> 26. Is the music technically, aesthetically, and expressively good? This judgment is basic and primary and should be made by competent musicians. Only artistically sound music will be effective in the long run. To admit the cheap, the trite, the musical cliché often found in popular songs

for the purpose of "instant liturgy" is to cheapen the liturgy, to expose it to ridicule, and to invite failure.

Three problems immediately arise from this article's assertions. First, how does one determine that music is "technically, aesthetically, and expressively good"? At a technical level, one may judge that parallel fifths are to be reprobated in sixteenth-century hymn harmonizations but applauded in Bartok and Debussy, that repeated harmonic patterns are evidence of poverty of musical invention in Boccherini or Rossini but highly creative in Glass or Pärt, that "Ah-men" is the correct pronunciation of the Hebrew term when performing one of Handel's oratorios but "Aye-men" when performing a spiritual, etc. At an aesthetic level, one may judge both the total determinacy of a piece of electronic music and the total indeterminacy of a piece by John Cage aesthetically proper, not to speak of the quasi-mathematical perfection of a Bach prelude and fugue or the episodic yearning of a late Mahler symphony. At an expressive level, does one pit the sound of the Mormon Tabernacle Choir against the Anonymous 4 (and both against the sound of Shape-Note singers), or Luciano Pavarotti against Aretha Franklin (and both against a mother crooning a lullabye to her child) to determine what is "good"?

Second, how does one determine who are the competent musicians able to make this determination? Even if one were musically competent to judge the varying productions within a given culture (e.g., a Western musician displaying equal sensitivity and discrimination in evaluating a piece of Ars Nova polyphony, an Ornette Coleman improvisation, and a cut from the latest Toad the Wet Sprocket CD), could one also claim to judge the productions of another culture (e.g., an Indian raga, an Indonesian folk chorus, or a Balinese gamelin orchestra's improvisation)?

Third, what are the criteria by which competent musicians could determine what is cheap, trite, and cliché? Classical musicians such as Carl Orff and Paul Hindemith have lauded "Gebrauchmusik" that other classical musicians would consider trite; liturgical music theoreticians such as Bernard Huijbers and Tony Barr have emphasized the need for repetitive sequences in assembly-based singing, sequences some critics would call cliché.

Perhaps recognizing the difficulty in judging musical quality called for in MCW 27, its succeeding article distinguishes between the judgment of musical *value* and that of musical *style:*

> 28. We do a disservice to musical values, however, when we confuse the judgment of music with the judgment of musical style. Style and value are two distinct judgments. Good music of new styles is finding a happy

home in the celebrations of today. To chant and polyphony we have effectively added the chorale hymn, restored responsorial singing to some extent, and employed many styles of contemporary composition. Music in folk idiom is finding acceptance in eucharistic celebrations. We must judge value within each style. . . .

While this distinction may overcome some of the difficulties noted above, it remains problematic and will be expressly rejected by SS [see below].

Presuming that only pieces judged musically good by competent musicians will be admitted for Roman Rite worship, MCW outlines the other components of the threefold judgment that must be made, since "not all good music is suitable to the liturgy" (MCW 29). MCW asserts that the good music chosen can be judged as liturgically appropriate by reference to the liturgy's structure, texts, and role differentiations.

Liturgically appropriate music must communicate and enhance the differing ritual importance of various elements in Roman Rite worship:

31. The choice of sung parts, the balance between them, and the style of musical setting used should reflect the relative importance of the parts of the Mass (or other service) and the nature of each part. . . .

At first glance this structural requirement seems to suggest that the ritual weight of each element of a liturgical service should be matched by the elaborateness of the music employed. For example, since GIRM 54 declares that the Eucharistic Prayer is "the center and summit of the entire celebration," it should always have the most extensive musical elaboration of any element in the Mass. Conversely, since GIRM 24 declares that the introductory rites at Eucharist "have the character of a beginning, introduction and preparation," they should be musically unelaborated. But such a simple correlation between ritual importance and musical elaboration does not take into account other ritual encoding (e.g., the Roman Rite sometimes signals the highest ritual importance by stopping all music, as when it directs that the laying on of hands at an ordination rite take place in silence) or the larger ritual structures ("macro-units") into which individual elements are placed.

Strongly emphasizing the logocentric character of Roman Rite worship music, MCW further asserts that liturgically appropriate music must clarify and not obscure the worship texts it sets:

32. Does the music express and interpret the text correctly and make it more meaningful? Is the form of the text respected? In making these judgments the principal classes of texts must be kept in mind: proclamations, acclamations, psalms and hymns, and prayers. Each has a specific function which must be served by the music chosen for a text. . . .

While all might agree that appropriate music must serve the liturgical text, determining precisely how it does so is quite complex.

What are the criteria by which one would determine if a given piece of music expresses a text correctly? Must the music conform to the accentual pattern of the spoken text or may the word accents be modified or distorted in a given setting for expressive purposes? Many Gregorian chants exhibit elaborate melismas on unaccented syllables while word accents receive less melodic attention: Do they express the text incorrectly? (Of course, one might ask the further question of why this would be important if most of the assembly members do not understand the language being sung anyway.) Cantillation formulae respect the accentual and syntactical patterns of the liturgical text (indeed, they might be considered "heightened speech"), but they do not codify shifts in conceptual content or mood (e.g., the same formula is used for the preface, whether the text speaks of the penitential practices of Lent, the jubilation of Easter, the veneration of the Blessed Virgin Mary, or Christian hope in the face of physical death at the funeral). Does this mean that cantillation formulae express texts correctly but interpret them poorly?

What musical codes are operative in interpreting a given text? For example, in Euro-American culture are certain modes or keys identified with particular emotional states (e.g., minor keys are sad, major keys are happy)? Are important words or syllables signaled by setting more notes to them than less important words or syllables (e.g., the "jubilus" of a chant Alleluia on the name of God)? Do certain meters and rhythms encode contrasting interpretations (e.g., slow melodies with held notes indicating grave topics and fast melodies with quick notes indicating levity)? Should varying timbres be employed to illustrate differing ideas in the texts? How do these codes and others like them operate in tandem or in opposition to signal the conceptual complexity and symbolic multivalence of liturgical texts (e.g., "O happy fault, O necessary sin of Adam," "The Lord reigns from the tree")?

What are the criteria by which one can determine if a liturgical form is being respected musically? How much repetition can a given phrase or text bear in a musical setting before it distorts or destroys the liturgical form (e.g., the lengthy "dona nobis pacem" movement at the end of the "Agnus Dei" in Haydn's *Paukenmesse*)? What should the musical setting do when the liturgical form conflicts with the canonical biblical form (as, for example, in settings of the responsorial psalm for Palm/Passion Sunday when the progress of thought from description of affliction to declaration of God's faithfulness is undermined by the recurrent refrain "My God, my God, why have you abandoned me?")? When composers set an Agnus Dei as a closed musical form without providing for varying lengths depending on the time it takes to accomplish the Fraction Rite, or when they compose a setting of the Lord's Prayer for use at Eucharist without dealing with the presidential invitation and embolism and the assembly's concluding acclamation, are they respecting the liturgical form?

MCW further states that, in addition to clarifying liturgical structure and enhancing liturgical texts, Roman Rite worship music must respect role differentiations in the liturgical assembly:

> 33. "In liturgical celebrations each one, minister or layperson, who has an office to perform, should do all of, but only, those parts which pertain to that office by the nature of the rite and the principles of liturgy." [CSL 28.] Special musical concern must be given to the role of the congregation, the cantor, the choir, and the instrumentalists.

How much freedom is allowed the composer in producing worship music for these various forces and by what criteria should the compositions be judged? In order to increase the opportunities for active congregational vocal participation, may a given musical setting detach a phrase from a liturgical text in order to create a congregational refrain (as, for example, in settings of the "Glory to God" where repetition of the opening phrases or sentence turn a *psalmos idiotikos* into a refrain/verse structure or when congregational interventions are inserted into the Exsultet proclamation)? While few would dispute that the verses of the responsorial psalm may be sung by a cantor/psalmist and/or by a choir, is it permissible for a composer to set these texts as an art song for cantor or anthem for choir without any opportunity for active congregational vocal participation? May a composer insert unprescribed congregational, cantorial, and/or choral interventions into a presidential text (e.g., having the congregation sing "We praise you, we bless you, we thank you" at various points during the Eucharistic Prayer in response to the cantor's sung cue or having the choir sing "Miserere nobis" under the intercessory sections of the prayer or echo presidential phrases in the preface or doxology)? When may instrumental music substitute for (e.g., an instrumental wedding processional rather than the prescribed *antiphona ad introitum*), underpin (e.g., an improvisation played under a spoken Blessing of Baptismal Water during the Rite of Baptism of Infants), or yoke (e.g., an interlude bridging between the "Lord have mercy" and "Glory to God" while the presiding celebrant recites his quasi-absolution text) liturgical texts and units?

Presuming that good music judged so by competent musicians has been further determined as liturgically appropriate by reference to its conformity to liturgical structures, its enhancement of liturgical texts, and its respect for liturgical role differentiation, MCW declares that it must also be pastorally fitting:

> 39. The pastoral judgment governs the use and function of every element of celebration. . . . It is the judgment that must be made in this particular situation, in these concrete circumstances. Does music in the celebration enable these people to express their faith, in this place, in this age, in this culture?

> 41. A musician may judge that a certain composition or style of composition is good music, but this musical judgment really says nothing about whether and how this music is to be used in this celebration. The signs of the celebration must be accepted and received as meaningful for a genuinely human faith experience for these specific worshipers. This pastoral judgment can be aided by sensitivity to the cultural and social characteristics of the people who make up the congregation: their age, culture, and education. These factors influence the effectiveness of the liturgical signs, including music. No set of rubrics or regulations of itself will ever achieve a truly pastoral celebration of the sacramental rites. Such regulations must always be applied with a pastoral concern for the given worshiping community.

Recognizing the complexity of attempting to determine the pastoral utility of a good music intended for Roman Rite liturgical music, MCW singles out three factors: the age, culture, and education of the worshipers. All three are problematic.

Studies in musical psychology demonstrate that capacities to perceive, reproduce, and appreciate music develop over time and in stages, reaching a plateau (except in professionally trained musicians) in late adolescence/young adulthood. Thus if one intends children to function as cantors, choir-members, and instrumentalists at eucharistic liturgies where their peers make up the majority of the worshiping assembly, as the *Directory for Masses with Children* suggests,[1] the music chosen must be age- and skill-level appropriate. In spite of popular media presentations in which certain musical styles are said to mark youth culture and others produce golden oldies, age by itself does not seem to determine one's ability to appreciate a particular musical style: senior citizens may enjoy a Beatles tune while twenty-somethings may powerfully respond to chant. Although there may be circumstances in which a particular musical idiom ostensibly appealing to a particular age group might be employed at Roman Rite worship, the fact that the liturgy normally gathers worshipers of diverse ages suggests that music should be chosen to allow active participation by many age groups.

Studies in musical sociology demonstrate that particular styles of music may encode social identity. Thus stereotypically in U.S. culture, rap is identified as the music of alienated African-American urban males, country as the music of poor and working class whites, opera as the music of upper class elites. In fact marketing and mass media have done much to break down these stereotypical identifications; white suburban females groove to rap CDs, country performers fill stadiums and lounges at prices more representative of the middle class than the working poor, and opera draws passionate supporters (and detractors) from all socioeconomic ranks. Musical markers of social identity can become especially vexing in multicultural parishes when the music minister may not be sensitive to the varying cultural codes operative within a given language group (e.g., an Anglo musician programing Hispanic music without recognizing the diversity of Puerto Rican, Cuban, Mexican, and Central or South American styles). Pastoral difficulties may occur in at least two directions: (1) when the music chosen for common worship is so identified with a particular subculture not strongly represented in the worshiping assembly that it causes discomfort in the assembled worshipers; and (2) when the music chosen for common worship is so divorced from the worshipers' musical culture that it alienates the assembled worshipers.

Common wisdom suggests that the higher the level of education the more sophisticated the appreciation of musical variety. However, with the increasing specialization of higher education in the United States, one may become quite educated in the sciences or one's profession without being correspondingly developed in the fine arts and the humanities. Thus it cannot be assumed that the worshipers in a university campus ministry program will express their faith with the artistic monuments of the Western classical music tradition. Conversely with the educational opportunities provided by the mass media, those without formal schooling may express their faith in an astonishing variety of musical idioms. Therefore, considering only the worshipers' formal educational background may mislead those determining the liturgical music program.

Thus the pastoral dimension of the threefold musical judgment may be assisted by considering the worshipers' ages, culture, and education, but more sophisticated criteria are needed. With its emphasis on liturgical music as the self-expression of the gathered worshipers, MCW neglects the prophetic dimension of worship music. In the long run a liturgical music program may transform an assembly's talents and tastes, leading the worshipers beyond their perceived capabilities and preferences to other experiences of the transcendent in sound. How the diversity of musical tastes occurring in worshiping assemblies is to be identified, accommodated, critiqued, and/or transformed remains a strong challenge in exercising the pastoral dimension of

MCW's threefold judgment of the qualities needed in Roman Rite worship music.

The Milwaukee Report

Since LMT does not discuss the qualities demanded by Roman Rite worship music, MR's discussion of these qualities appears as a series of refinements (art. 81) of MCW's treatment. These refinements include comments on the unity of the threefold judgment, the competence of those called to exercise this judgment, the need to contextualize the judgment of any individual musical element, the necessity of judging music in performance rather than simply from graphic representations, and the cultural underpinnings of any attempt to determine the qualities appropriate for Roman Rite worship music.

We noted above the problem created by MCW's treatment of the threefold judgment as three separate determinations hierarchically gradated. MR specifies some of the problems arising from this approach:

> 82. One difficulty is the tendency to treat the musical-liturgical-pastoral judgment as three separate judgments. In its introduction to the sections on this topic, MCW notes that "a threefold judgment must be made: musical, liturgical and pastoral." Yet the ensuing sections of MCW contribute to a fragmentation of this single, multifaceted judgment by treating the musical, liturgical and pastoral aspects separately, without any discussion of their integration. This presentation has given the impression that there is a chronological progression to these judgments, with priority given to the final (pastoral) judgment. Thus the various judgments—especially the musical and the pastoral—are sometimes perceived to be in opposition to each other. To avoid such conflicts and to respect more completely the formulation found in MCW, it is necessary to admit of a single, multifaceted judgment for evaluating musical elements in worship. A model for this can be found in E[nvironment and] A[rt in] C[atholic] W[orship], whose standards of quality and appropriateness are distinctive yet complementary. Acknowledging the need for an integrated judgment requires a balancing of the various facets of this single judgment and not the opposition of one element to another. The process of the judgment, therefore, is not chronological but dynamic and interactive.

The difficulties engendered by dividing and hierarchically gradating the three aspects of this single judgment are only exacerbated when they are separated over time and by personnel. Situations in which the judgments of the musician and liturgical coordinator are regularly overturned by clergy who claim sole pastoral competence are as frustrating as those in which clergy must suffer choices imposed by the liturgical coordinator and musician oblivious to the life concerns of the worshipers. If this single judgment is to integrate musical, liturgical, and pastoral perspectives in a single dynamic and interactive process, those called on to exercise this judgment must likewise integrate these perspectives. As MR notes:

> 83. One step toward integrating the various facets of the musical-liturgical-pastoral judgment is an integration of the various perspectives and peoples involved. For example, MCW notes the judgments about the technical, aesthetic and expressive quality of a musical work should be made by a competent musician. Professional musicians bring a wealth of information and experience to the task of judging the quality of a musical work. Yet, people who are not trained musicians also have much to say about the quality of worship music. On the one hand, while detailing the nature of the pastoral judgment, MCW notes that although a musician may judge that a certain work is good music, this judgment says nothing about whether or how this music is to be used in worship. Some have drawn the questionable conclusion from this statement that the pastoral judgment can be made apart from the musical one, and by people other than the musician. Yet, just as people who are not trained musicians have something to contribute when assessing the quality of worship music, so do musical professionals have something to say about the pastoral selection and use of such music. The integration of various people and perspectives in all facets of the musical-liturgical-pastoral judgment is required if the integrity of that judgment is to be respected and promoted.

MR strongly criticizes MCW's framework for judging individual pieces of worship music seemingly without reference to the entire ritual experience:

> 84. An integrated approach to the musical-liturgical-pastoral judgment demonstrates that no single musical element can be evaluated apart from the whole of the liturgical-musical contour. The principles for liturgical preparation articulated above noted that no one aspect of the worship event should be prepared in isolation from the other elements. Similarly, a single musical element cannot adequately be evaluated apart from the larger musical-liturgical context. It is not possible to evaluate a setting of the Holy, for example, without considering the rest of the eucharistic acclamations, as well as the larger musical-liturgical contour of the Liturgy of the Eucharist. Considering the musical-liturgical-pastoral merits of the various musical components in view of each other is thus an important step toward achieving an integrated musical-liturgical-pastoral judgment on the worship music.

The concern expressed in this article is easily illustrated by a musical program for a Lord's Day Eucharist during the Easter season in which the opening processional music is the congregational hymn "I Know That My Redeemer Lives," the "Lord Have Mercy" is the "Kyrie

Eleison" from the Missa Lux et origo (sung in alternation by schola and assembly), and the "Glory to God" is the "Gloria in excelsis" from the Mozart "Coronation" Mass sung by choir and soloists. Each of the pieces of music in this hypothetical program would pass MCW's threefold judgment as being musically well-crafted, liturgically correct, and pastorally appropriate, yet when they are yoked with each other the result is ritually problematic: an over-weighting of the introductory rites. In adding a ritual dimension to the threefold judgment, MR asserts that pastoral planners must be concerned not only with slot filling, but with macro-unit structuring.

MR supplements the musical dimension of MCW's threefold judgment with attention to its performative aspect:

> 85. The dynamic nature of the worship event also suggests that the musical-liturgical-pastoral evaluation of the worship music must take into account the performance of the music in the liturgy, and not simply evaluate the music in its printed form. A common Western bias is that one can judge a composition according to what is in the score and, when appropriate, offer a separate judgment about the quality of the musicians or of the musical performance. When considering Christian ritual music, however, these judgments need to be fused. This fusion of the compositional and performative aspects of a piece is necessary because the quality of a work is influenced by its context. One element comprising that context is the performance. Furthermore, some ritual composition—such as the music of Taizé or most gospel music—is constructed to be improvised. Evaluating such music simply by analyzing what appears on the page is, therefore, inadequate.

MR's stance raises some interesting questions for liturgical music aesthetics. Is it appropriate to judge the performance of worship music by the same standards one would apply to a concert performance, since the contexts (worship vs. artistic engagement) are different if not opposed? If not, what criteria are to be employed in determining (even in performance) good, appropriate, and/or effective worship music from bad, inappropriate, and/or ineffective worship music? If one removes oneself from the worship experience enough to gain the aesthetic distance to offer a critique of the music, has one refused the invitation to engage in full, conscious, and active participation in the ritual prayer?

The final addition MR makes to MCW's threefold judgment is a cultural aspect:

> 86. Of all the contexts influencing this musical-liturgical-pastoral judgment, the cultural one is the most decisive. Different cultures, language groups, and ethnic communities provide different contexts and raise particular questions when rendering the musical-liturgical-pastoral judgment

about worship music. It is important to respect each culture that provides the context for the musical-liturgical-pastoral judgment. This entails consciously avoiding the ethnocentrism that judges the music of one particular culture and era as superior and the model for all other Christian ritual music. To avoid this hazard, it is indispensable that appropriate representatives of those cultures providing the context for worship be central to the decision-making process. In particular, it is important to engage competent musicians, versed in the music of the cultures providing the context for worship. They will be key in helping their colleagues, especially in the musical facet of the musical-liturgical-pastoral judgment.

While this article decries possible cultural imperialism manifest in a worship music program, it must also contend with the possibility of transcultural interchange and mutual influence. Especially under the influence of the mass media, musical cultures assimilate influences from a wide variety of sources; worship music cultures are no different. For example, white Catholic congregations may sing "Were You There When They Crucified My Lord?" with deep conviction on Palm/Passion Sunday or Good Friday, though with timbre and style quite different than an African-American congregation; "Pescador de Hombres" is sung (in Spanish or in English translation) by many Anglo communities, though without the characteristic instrumentation of the original; and various African and Asian melodies have been adorned with English texts as worship songs as part of a general "world music" movement. On the other hand, the cultural connotations of particular melodies, timbres, rhythms, or instruments may be incapable of assimilation and thus impede worship. Although the melody "The Yellow Rose of Texas" is in 8686D meter, it would be difficult in the English-speaking United States to sing a hymn text written in that meter to the tune because of its extra-liturgical connotations. Just as some Catholic worshipers were shocked when guitars were introduced as accompaniment instruments in Roman Rite worship in the 1960s, so others may be shocked today by accordions at a so-called polka Mass or a bank of synthesizers at a youth Mass. MR's emphasis on the cultural context for judging appropriate Roman Rite worship music both clarifies and complexifies the pastoral dimension of MCW's threefold judgment.

The Snowbird Statement

A great contrast appears between SS and MR in the treatment of the qualities appropriate to Roman Catholic worship music. While both documents accept the framework for judgment proffered in

MCW, SS treats the musical, liturgical, and pastoral judgments as three separate activities rather than three aspects of a single activity:

> 6. In 1972, the U.S. Bishops' Committee on the Liturgy issued the docu-
> ment *Music in Catholic Worship* which established that three judgments
> should determine the appropriateness of music for liturgy: the musical
> judgment, the pastoral judgment, and the liturgical judgment. Various at-
> tempts have been made to refine the criteria for these judgments and to
> integrate their diverse concerns. We welcome the considerable progress
> made in advancing the criteria for the pastoral and liturgical judgments.
> We note, however, the inadequate development of criteria for the musical
> judgment. Given the current lack of consensus in the church on what con-
> stitutes "good" music, and even the lack of serious discussion of this
> issue, efforts to correlate the three judgments cannot help but remain un-
> satisfactory.

This conceptualization influences all subsequent discussion in SS.

Having asserted that criteria for judging the liturgical and pastoral appropriateness of particular pieces of music in Roman Rite worship are well developed, SS devotes itself to developing criteria for making a judgment of musical worth. It takes quite different positions from MR on these criteria and on who is competent to make such judgments:

> [6.] As a stimulus for discussion on this matter, we propose the following
> about the musical judgment: some music is of higher quality than others;
> not all music is good. Certainly, musical standards are not absolute or un-
> changing, and church history attests this mutability. Still, we are con-
> vinced that the elements which comprise the musical judgment are
> objective and are something more than mere assertions of personal pref-
> erence or of social or historical convention. There are those who, through
> training and talent, are able to identify music that is technically, aestheti-
> cally and expressively good. In seeking to judge musical quality, we do
> well to consult the cumulative wisdom of both our contemporaries and
> predecessors.

SS acknowledges the difficulty in identifying positive criteria by which music may be judged technically, aesthetically, and expressively good, but asserts that simply because it is incapable of identifying such criteria at the present time is no reason to believe that they do not exist. SS directly rejects MCW's (and by extension MR's) declaration that the value of a piece of music must be judged within its style:

> [6.] In asserting the objectivity of judgments about musical quality, we are
> consciously rejecting relativistic positions. We do not think that the mod-
> ern cultural situation renders musical evaluation impossible or compels
> the avoidance of the issue of musical quality. We do not share the often
> asserted opinion that comparison is valid only within a particular style.

To the extent that many of the styles employed in English-language Catholic worship today are dialects of the same larger musical language (in terms of harmonic vocabulary or rhythmic organization), a discussion of musical quality across stylistic boundaries is valid and necessary. The difficulty of definitively stating the objective elements of musical quality is not an excuse for avoiding the issue or proof of the relativity of musical judgments, but rather an indication of human incompleteness and an impetus to further conversation.

Perhaps SS's strongest assertion lies in its claim that there is a characteristic ethos of Catholic liturgical music, although the statement acknowledges how difficult it is to define this ethos:

8. We believe that there exists a characteristic ethos of Catholic liturgical music, although we acknowledge that such is difficult to define. To identify the ethos narrowly with any specific period or genre in liturgical-musical history would be a mistake. The church is not intrinsically limited to any particular "sacred" style of music for the celebration of the liturgy. Still, we believe that a Catholic ethos is discernable, for instance, in music that elaborates the sacramental mysteries in a manner attentive to the public, cosmic and transcendent character of religion, rather than in styles of music that are overly personalized, introverted or privatized. Music employed by countless generations of Catholic Christians is the starting point for discerning the characteristics of a Catholic ethos in liturgical music. In response to the church's developing needs and the many new cultural contexts within which the church worships, the ethos of Catholic liturgical music will continue to find new expressions. This process of development, however, should consult pre-existing forms to a greater extent than has generally been the case in recent decades. We advocate that new forms and styles grow organically from extant forms which display a Catholic ethos. We seek to articulate more objectively the characteristics of the Catholic ethos which we intuitively believe to exist.

Note that SS distances itself from the teaching of TLS that identifies the ethos of Catholic worship music with Gregorian chant, classical polyphony, and more modern music in descending value. But once again the question of the criteria by which one is to determine which music "elaborates the sacramental mysteries in a manner attentive to the public, cosmic and transcendent character of religion" signals the difficulty SS acknowledges in determining what is a distinctively Catholic ethos of worship music. Although the liturgical music of various Orthodox Christian communities would fulfill the criterion listed above, I suspect SS would not judge this music as part of the distinctive ethos of Catholic worship music.

A similar difficulty attends SS's recommendation that compositions demonstrating this Catholic ethos serve as models for contemporary and future liturgical music compositions. For example, the force of the eschatological text of the end of the preface as well as the rubrics of the GIRM counsel that the Sanctus should be vocally executed by the entire assembly with the presiding priest. While some Gregorian chant settings of the Sanctus seem simple enough for congregational singing, the complexity of others seems to demand performance by a schola or choir. A mode five chant assigned in various manuscripts for solemn or semi-double feasts serves as the basis for the tenor line of the Sanctus in Guillaume de Machaut's *Messe de Nostre Dame* (ca. 1360), but the pattern of this chant has been transformed isorhythmically and surrounded by three other voices. No congregational line appears in the composition and its performance demands trained singers. In the Joseph Haydn *Paukenmesse* the Sanctus text has been split into multiple musical movements ("Sanctus, Sanctus, Sanctus, Dominus Deus Sabaoth": an *Adagio* for alto solo and full chorus; "Pleni sunt coeli et terra gloria tua": an *Allegro con spiritu* for full chorus, followed by "Osanna in excelsis" for alto solo and full chorus; "Benedictus qui venit in nomine Domini": an *Andante* for solo vocal quartet, followed by "Osanna in excelsis" for solo quartet and full chorus) accompanied by two oboes (or clarinets), two bassoons, two trumpets, two trombones, timpani, two violins, viola, cello, bass, and organ. Again no congregational participation is indicated and trained singers and instrumentalists are necessary to execute the music. Which of the above-mentioned compositions represent a genuine "Catholic ethos" of worship music that should serve as the basis for consultation and from which new compositions should organically develop?

Consistent with SS's espousal of an objectivist position is its call for excellence in all aspects of Roman Rite worship music:

> 4. We wish to affirm standards of excellence in the composition and performance of all musical forms in the church's liturgy: choral, cantorial, diaconal, presidential and instrumental. There is no necessary inconsistency between traditional standards of excellence and the pastoral principles of the renewed liturgy; nor does sound liturgical theology suggest such a discrepancy. Where standards of excellence exist in theory or in practice they should be sustained; where they do not exist, they should be developed and fostered.

Although it acknowledges some of the difficulties involved in positing definitive criteria by which a piece of music may be judged technically, aesthetically, and expressively good, SS does offer criteria by which a piece of music may be judged bad, qualities associated with what it terms the "entertainment or therapeutic ethos":

7. While we believe that the process of dialogue between liturgy and its cultural context must be promoted and advanced, we challenge the indiscriminate incorporation of an entertainment or therapeutic ethos into liturgical music. We think that this development constitutes one of the most serious problems in the present moment of the church's liturgical life. Particular dangers inherent in the adoption of currently popular musical styles and idioms are sentimentality, consumerism, individualism, introversion and passivity. Means for evaluating various musical styles and expressions must be generated in order to avoid these particularly pervasive tendencies.

Judging the five particular dangers associated by SS with the use of popular musical styles and idioms in Roman Rite worship music is complicated by the fact that these qualities are manifest in different cultural codes. Sentimentality (presumably an illegitimate manipulation of emotion) may mark text and/or music in a given liturgical composition, but determining its contours is notoriously difficult: what may be perceived as heartfelt emotion in one cultural or ritual context could be perceived as maudlin claptrap in another. Consumerism does not so much qualify liturgical text and/or music itself as the marketing strategies and economic structures by which these compositions are provided to liturgical planners and worshiping communities; presumably SS here critiques the packaging of liturgical composers as star performers of their own compositions and the advertising pressures placed on worshiping communities to buy the latest new compositions at the expense of developing a stable repertoire. Individualism may be manifest in texts (overusing the first person singular in corporate song), music (programing styles so that personal tastes are assuaged), or leadership strategies (performing for a congregation rather than enabling the assembly's sung prayer). Introversion would tag not so much particular compositions as the effect they have upon performers/listeners; presumably SS here excoriates so-called mood music employed in the liturgy to create an ambient sonic environment rather than to vigorously assert faith. Passivity would similarly not inhere in particular compositions as in the performers/listeners who engage them; insofar as Roman Rite worship music obscures the challenge of gospel living or lulls worshipers with an aura of religiosity, it contradicts SC's call for full, conscious, and active participation of the faithful in the liturgical event. One could assert, however, that folk- and art-music compositions may also betray these characteristics (e.g., Victorian or Edwardian hymnody, recital series and choral workshops, newspaper advertisements of the music program being sung at a worship service, organ improvisations and interludes during the course of a liturgy, and programming that silences the assembly in favor of choral and soloists' artistry may equally be accused of sentimentality, consumerism, individualism, introversion, and/or passivity).

Over the course of this chapter we have seen a marked change in the evaluation of the qualities deemed necessary for Roman Rite worship music.

While "holiness" remains a prime desideratum in Roman Rite worship music, this holiness is increasingly conceptualized functionally rather than ontologically. It is neither music in and of itself nor particular elements of music (such as its tonal organization, volume, rhythm, timbre, etc.) that manifest holiness; rather, worship music is holy insofar as it sustains and supports the action of the liturgy. Whatever music facilitates the ritual prayer of a given assembly partakes of the liturgy's holiness; conversely whatever music impedes or distracts from common prayer falls from holiness.

The documents we have studied have also listed "universality" as a desirable quality in Roman Rite worship music, but the understanding of universality has shifted: from music that gives no offense to strangers, through music that allows members of the Roman Rite to feel at home wherever they may be, to music that gives expression to the religious experience of varying cultures that make up the worshiping assembly and connects contemporary worshipers with their forebears in the faith.

According to the documents studied, Roman Rite worship music must be true art. Initially the documents found it necessary to defend the artistic integrity of chant and Roman school polyphony. Later documents grounded the assessment of worship music as art in the context of an overarching teleological understanding of artistic creation. More recent documents agree that all Roman Rite worship music must be technically, aesthetically, and expressively good, but contrast pluralist ethnomusicological perspectives with classicist aesthetic perspectives on what constitutes good music.

Roman Rite worship music must also bear the quality of ritual appropriateness. Earlier documents declared that the musical setting of each element must respect its relative ritual importance, its officially designated text, and the minister(s) performing it. Later documents especially emphasized that the musical form must respect the ritual function. The most recent documents evidence a concern that the music chosen not only fit the individual moments of the ritual, but genuinely contribute to the ritual flow.

Finally, Roman Rite worship music must be pastorally effective. Earlier documents claimed that such effectiveness could be guaranteed by a standardized repertoire primarily consisting of Gregorian chant and Roman school polyphony. Later documents sketched how music might contribute to both internal and external liturgical participation by members of the worshiping assembly. The most recent documents advert to the complexity of determining pastorally effective Roman Rite worship music, noting that factors such as the age, culture, and education of the worshipers must be taken into account.

Having traced these shifts in understanding of the definition, purpose, and essential qualities of Roman Rite worship music in the twentieth century, we now consider shifts in understanding of the persons who produce and are responsible for Roman Rite worship music.

ENDNOTE

[1] "22. The principles of active and conscious participation are in a sense even more significant for Masses celebrated with children. . . . For this reason as many children as possible should have special parts in the celebration: for example, . . . acting as cantor . . . , singing in a choir, playing musical instruments. . . . In all this, it should be kept in mind that external activities will be fruitless and even harmful if they do not serve the internal participation of the children. . . .

"24 . . . Even in Masses with children attention is to be paid to the diversity of ministries so that the Mass may stand out clearly as the celebration of a community. For example, readers and cantors, whether children or adults, should be employed. . . .

"32. The use of 'musical instruments can add a great deal' in Masses with children, especially if they are played by the children themselves."

4

What People Are to Make Roman Catholic Worship Music?

The nine documents we are examining present varying perspectives on what constitutes Roman Catholic worship music, what its purpose and functions are, and what qualities it must exhibit. It is therefore not surprising to discover that they also exhibit a variety of understandings of and prescriptions concerning the people who execute Roman Catholic worship music.

Tra le sollecitudini

Just as it founded our consideration of the nature, purpose, and qualities of Roman Catholic worship music, so TLS offers an initial framework for considering the people who should make it:

> 12. Except the chant of the celebrant and the sacred ministers at the altar, which must always be sung in Gregorian chant without accompaniment, the rest of the liturgical singing belongs properly to the choir of clerics; wherefore singers in the church, if they are laymen, are the substitutes of the ecclesiastical choir. Hence their music, at any rate for the greater part, must keep the nature of choir music.

Consistent with its understanding of Roman Rite liturgical music as a logocentric act of the Church, TLS emphasizes that the people who perform it should do so as members of a collective body that has a distinctly clerical character. TLS seems to offer another criterion by which to determine genuine liturgical music, in addition to genre, language, purpose, and setting: it should be sung by a clerical choir. There is some historical justification for such a view, since by the time of the *Ordo Romanus Primus* music chanted at the papal Mass was primarily the responsibility of a "professional" group of clerics (the *schola cantorum*) with their own officers, and later Roman Rite documents simply assume this custom.

The reasoning that declares that nonclerics can substitute for clerics in a liturgical choir raises a variety of issues. If the singing of the choir is a genuinely liturgical act, can a nonbaptized person be a member of such a choir, since by common Catholic teaching it is baptism that renders an individual capable of liturgical worship? Can nonclerics assume other properly clerical roles at liturgy? If so, which roles and why? Do nonchoir members of the assembly exercise a genuine liturgical function when they join in the chants of the choir, or are they simply enhancing the sound?

Such a conceptualization of the people who perform Roman Rite liturgical music leads TLS to three practical consequences. First, the clerical or quasi-clerical choir of singers performs its ministry collectively rather than as individuals:

> [12.] This does not entirely exclude solos. But these must never take the chief place in a service, they should never absorb the greater part of the liturgical text: they must be rather points of musical emphasis and accent bound up closely with the rest of the composition which should remain strictly choral.

Note that the article does not really address the role of cantors in Roman Rite worship music, whether intoning the initial melodies for choral singing or chanting the invocations of a litany. It simply challenges the practice of certain Baroque, Classical, and Romantic art music composers to construe segments of liturgical texts as arias, duets, trios, quartets, etc.

Second, TLS reasons that if the clerical or quasi-clerical choir of singers performs a genuinely "priestly" action within the liturgical service and if women as such are incapable of exercising such priestly action, women cannot be members of a liturgical choir:

> 13. It follows from the same principle that the singers in church have a real liturgical office, and that women, therefore, being incapable of such an office, cannot be admitted to the choir. If high voices, such as treble and alto, are wanted, these parts must be sung by boys, according to the ancient custom of the Church.

This reasoning leads to certain theoretical and practical difficulties. First, what is the role of the choir in an all-female liturgical community such as an enclosed group of nuns or sisters where the only priestly figure is the ordained celebrant? Second, while this reasoning supports the maintenance of boy choirs with excellent educational and cultural consequences both for the boys in the programs and for the communities that sustain them, it seems to discriminate unjustly against similar programs for girls. Third, such reasoning also provides justification for castrati as singers of Roman Rite worship music, but to contemporary minds it seems heinous that the desire for a particular vocal timbre could rationalize the sexual mutilation of boy singers.

Third, TLS asserts that the choir of singers should (positively) offer moral models to the rest of the assembly and (negatively) never distract them from their ritual prayer:

> 14. Lastly, only men of known piety and integrity who, by their modest and reverent demeanor during the service show themselves worthy of the sacred duty they perform, may be allowed to sing in the church. It would also be more suitable if the singers, while they are in choir, were to wear cassocks and surplices; and if their place be too much exposed to the gaze of the people, it should be guarded by a grating.

TLS's suggestion that choir members be dressed in clerical garb (cassocks and surplices) is consistent with liturgical customs that would dress presbyters in the vesture of another order if they were to play the role of deacon or sub-deacon at the solemn liturgy. But from a contemporary perspective, if choir vesture is desired, it would seem more authentic to robe them in albs, since these white robes represent the baptismal garments proper to the faithful rather than distinctively clerical vesture.

The concern that the choir members not be visually distracting to the other worshipers obliquely raises the question of the architectural placement of the choir. Four major models for placement of the choir appear in the history of the Roman Rite. The *Ordo Romanus Primus* indicates that members of the *schola cantorum* stood facing one another in two rows (adult males in the back, boys in the front) before the sanctuary in a basilical structure; the document does not indicate where these choir members sat (if they did so) when they were not singing. Many medieval Roman Rite structures developed choir stalls facing one another before the high altar in the sanctuary area itself, with the sanctuary separated from the nave by a screen of some sort. Some Roman Rite structures positioned the choir behind the high altar in the curvature of the apse. Finally, many Baroque and post-Baroque structures positioned the choir in a gallery elevated at the back of the nave, usually over the vestibule entry into the church. Each model signals a different solution to the acoustic, ritual, and symbolic demands placed on the choir's music ministry in the Roman Rite.

Although TLS begins the twentieth-century discussion of the appropriate people to execute Roman Rite worship music, its reflections reveal some surprising omissions. Although it elsewhere encourages active liturgical participation on the part of the baptized, it does not address the singing of assembly-members other than the choir during worship. It offers no guidelines for cantors other than the restrictive remarks it makes about soloists. It has no prescriptions for instrumentalists, directors, and coordinators of music programs for worshiping communities, text writers, or composers. However, later documents will address each of these groups with a variety of prescriptions and suggestions.

Musicae sacrae disciplina

MSD rescinds the restriction TLS placed on women serving in a liturgical choir, apparently modifying (though not discarding) the teaching that the choir may be a quasi-clerical entity:

> 74. Where it is impossible to have schools of singers or where there are not enough choir boys, it is allowed that a group of men and women or girls, located in a place outside the sanctuary set apart for the exclusive use of this group, can sing the liturgical texts at Solemn Mass, as long as the men are completely separated from the women and girls and everything unbecoming is avoided.

This article reveals certain biases. First, the use of female singers in a liturgical choir is seen as a last resort, tolerable only when males are unavailable. Second, no permission is granted for a liturgical choir completely composed of women, probably since MSD continues to conceive the musical choir as a substitute for a choir of clerics. (This interpretation is supported by the fact that the document demands that a mixed choir be located outside the sanctuary, presumably since the sanctuary space should only be accessible to clerics or potential clerics, i.e., males.) Third, while a grating shielding the assembly's visual perception of the choir is not mentioned, physical separation of the sexes is demanded. (Some architectural schemes went so far as to place the organ console in the midst of the choir space, physically segregating males from females who entered and exited the space by separate doors.) The concern that everything unbecoming be avoided echoes the teaching of TLS on the role of choir members as moral exemplars to the rest of the worshipers.

The 1958 Instruction

1958Inst is the first of the documents examined to offer a systematic set of definitions and guidelines for musical personnel in Roman

Rite worship. The document attempts to clarify the differing quality of liturgical participation exercised by various members of the worshiping assembly:

> 93. The *priest celebrant* presides at all liturgical functions. All others are to participate in the liturgical function in the manner proper to each.
>
> a. *Clerics,* who participate in liturgical functions in the manner and form prescribed by the rubrics, that is to say, as clerics, acting either as sacred ministers or in place of minor ministers, or even taking part in the choir or schola cantorum, *exercise a true and proper ministerial service* by virtue of their ordination and assumption of the clerical state.
>
> b. *The laity also exercise an active liturgical participation* by virtue of their baptismal character, because of which in the Holy Sacrifice of the Mass they offer in their own way, along with the priest, the divine victim to God the Father. . . .
>
> c. But the laity of male sex, whether children, youth, or men, when they are appointed by the competent ecclesiastical authority as ministers of the altar or to execute sacred music, if they fulfill such duties in the manner and form established by the rubrics, exercise a *direct but delegated ministerial service,* on the condition that, where they are to sing, they form an actual part of the "choir," the schola cantorum.

According to Inst1958, there are four categories of faithful engaging the liturgy. Ordained celebrants (bishops or presbyters) exercise the fullest liturgical participation by *presiding* over the liturgical assembly. In second place, clerics in major orders (at that time sub-deacons, deacons, presbyters, and bishops) or in minor orders (at that time porters, lectors, exorcists, and acolytes) exercise *direct ministerial service* (1) when they exercise their actual order (e.g., when a deacon proclaims the gospel); (2) when they substitute for another clerical order (e.g., when an ordained presbyter dresses in the vesture of and takes the role of a sub-deacon at solemn Mass); or (3) when they sing as members of the *schola cantorum.* In third place are male non-clerics who exercise *direct but delegated ministerial service;* perhaps the most familiar version of this service occurred when altar boys substituted for ordained acolytes, but male choir singers also fit this category. Finally, male non-clerics and females seem to exercise *genuine but indirect liturgical participation* in Roman Rite worship. Presumably in each category, the possibilities of internal, external, and sacramental participation remain in force. With reference to this final category, Inst1958 recognizes for the first time an all-female liturgical choir, but the sense that the liturgical choir substitutes for the properly clerical choir still influences the document's teaching about its architectural placement:

100. If in some place, a [choir of clerics or of laymen and boys alone] cannot be organized, the institution of a choir of the faithful is permitted, whether "mixed," or entirely of women or of girls only.

Such a choir should take its position in a convenient place, but outside the sanctuary or communion rail. In such a choir, too, the men should be separated from the women or girls, scrupulously avoiding anything that is not fitting.

Having established this framework, Inst1958 addresses five particular subcategories of the faithful involved in Roman Rite worship music: composers, organist-music directors, singers, instrumentalists, and commentators (although the last-named are not explicitly cited in 97–98):

97. All those who take part in sacred music, as composers, organists, choir directors, singers, or musicians, should above all give good example of Christian life to the rest of the faithful because they directly or indirectly participate in the sacred liturgy.

98. The same persons, besides bearing in mind the required excellence of faith and Christian morals, should possess a greater or lesser instruction in accordance with their circumstances and participation in the liturgy.

The role of moral exemplars that TLS and MSD had given to the choir now falls on all who exercise liturgical leadership. Inst1958 further presumes that technical formation is necessary in addition to good character and willingness to serve, a technical formation it sketches for each of the subcategories.

Those responsible for generating Roman Rite liturgical music form the first subcategory. They are termed authors or composers, but at the time Inst1958 was written genuinely liturgical music set prescribed liturgical texts in the sacred languages, leaving relatively little opportunity for authors to generate new liturgical texts. Nevertheless Inst1958 outlines the educational requirements for those producing liturgical compositions:

[98] a. *Authors* or *composers of sacred music* should possess sufficient knowledge of the sacred liturgy itself under its historical, dogmatic or doctrinal, practical or rubrical aspects. They should also know Latin. And, finally, they must have a sound training in the art of sacred and of profane music and in the history of music.

Liturgical composers and authors are expected to be educated in three areas: liturgy, linguistics, and music. Presumably historical knowledge of the liturgy will equip the composer with various models for textual/musical/ritual interaction with the strengths and weaknesses of each model clearly identified. Since the official Roman Rite liturgical texts at that time were primarily in Latin, one had to know the language not only to understand the meanings being conveyed, but the acoustic and accentual patterns to be respected by the musical settings. Finally, composers should be well-versed in musical theory with demonstrated skills in vocal and instrumental arrangement, as well as conversant with the monuments of both Christian and non-Christian musical traditions.

Those responsible for planning and directing worship music programs form the second subcategory. They are termed organists and choir directors, since in fact these two roles were often exercised by a single human being, although each role has distinct responsibilities:

> [98] b. *Organists* and *choir directors* must have a broad knowledge of the sacred liturgy and sufficient understanding of the Latin tongue. They should be experts also in their own art so that they will be able to fulfill their duty with competence and dignity.

Organists-choir directors are expected to show competence in the same three areas as worship music authors and composers, but without as extensive training.

Again responding to the traditionally logocentric character of Roman Rite worship music, singers form the third subcategory:

> [98] c. The *singers* too, children as well as adults, must be given such an understanding of the liturgical functions and texts that they are to sing, according to their capacity, that their song may go out from the intelligence of the mind as well as from the affection of the heart, as the "reasonable obedience" of their service demands. Let them also be trained to pronounce the Latin words correctly and distinctly. Rectors of churches and other responsible persons must see to it that there is good order in the part of the church occupied by the singers and that sincere devotion reigns there.

Since the choral singers at Roman Rite worship are not simply a glee club or concert performance group, Inst1958 demands that they sing with understanding. While the document judges it unreasonable to demand that every choir singer have the same knowledge of Latin required of a composer or choir director, each did have to learn the rules of pronunciation so that the texts would be properly proclaimed even if many in the assembly (or even in the choir) did not understand the text. Although it may strike a contemporary reader as odd that choir members would be taught how to properly pronounce individual syllables without understanding the words they were singing, note that not only adults but children as well made up the choir's membership. One could not expect facility in Latin from children who were frequently just learning the formal structures of their own vernacular language. Inst1958 recalls and heightens TLS's and MSD's concern for decorous behavior on the part of choir members.

Instrumentalists form the fourth subcategory in Inst1958's listing:

> [98] d. . . . *Instrumental musicians* who perform sacred music should not only be very expert in the technique of their own instrument but should also know well how to adapt its use to the laws of sacred music, and they should be so instructed in liturgical matters that they can harmoniously contribute the external exercise of their art with pious devotion.

Expectations of Latin linguistic facility apparently do not apply to instrumental musicians, but like the other subcategories they are expected to be liturgically informed as well as musically competent.

The final subcategory listed in Inst1958 officially recognizes a new role developed by European pastoral liturgists during the first half of the twentieth century to facilitate the assembly's external participation in the liturgy:

> 96. The active participation of the faithful, especially at Holy Mass and some more complex liturgical functions, can be more easily accomplished with the use of a "commentator." At the proper moment and in a few words, he can explain the rites and the prayers or lessons being read by the celebrant or his sacred ministers, and he can direct the external participation of the faithful—their responses, prayers, and songs.

What is fascinating from the vantage point of nearly forty years is the restriction placed on who might serve in this new quasi-clerical ministry:

> [96] a. It is fitting that the role of commentator may be performed by a priest or at least a cleric. When they cannot be had, the task may be entrusted to a layman of outstanding Christian life who is well instructed in his role. Women may never assume the role of commentator. It is only permitted that, in the case of necessity, a woman be used as director of the song and prayers of the faithful.

Note that, although women might not serve as commentators (for much the same reason that they could not earlier serve in a liturgical choir), they could serve as musical animators of the assembly, a function that will eventually be connected with the resurgence of the cantor's role in post-Vatican II worship. (The prayers of the faithful mentioned in this article are not the general intercessions restored to Roman Rite Eucharist in the aftermath of the Council, but a vernacular series of devotional petitionary prayers ["prone"] sometimes attached to preaching at Eucharist, other sacramental liturgies, and/or popular devotions.)

Having listed the foundational categories of those involved in making Roman Rite worship music and indicating the requirements and training for those involved in worship music leadership, Inst1958 also adverts to the remuneration worship music leaders might justly expect:

> 101. It is desirable that organists, choir directors, singers, musicians, and all others engaged in the service of the church offer their works of piety and of zeal for the love of God, without any recompense.
>
> Should it be that they are unable to offer their services gratuitously, Christian justice and charity demand that ecclesiastical superiors give them just pay, according to the various approved customs of the place and also in observance of the ordinances of civil laws.

This article obliquely recognizes a distinction between professional and volunteer worship music leadership that will complicate the practice of music ministry in many worshiping communities after the Vatican Council II.

Sacrosanctum Concilium

In earlier chapters we have noted that SC often simplified categories in which the discussion of Roman Rite worship had been carried on. For example, rather than the triple, quadruple, or quintuple categorization of Roman Catholic worship music proposed in earlier documents, SC speaks only of Gregorian chant and other forms of music. In much the same way, SC directly addresses only three categories of Roman Rite worship music makers: the assembly of the faithful, choirs, and composers. SC does not specifically treat the roles of clergy, cantors, organists, and instrumentalists or choir directors. The commentator's role is not mentioned, and that of the director of congregational song/prayers is not recognized as in Inst1958. Categories of professional and volunteer church musician appear nowhere in the Council's teaching:

> 114. . . . Choirs must be diligently promoted, especially in cathedral churches; but bishops and other pastors of souls must be at pains to ensure that whenever a liturgical service is to be celebrated with song, the whole assembly of the faithful is enabled . . . to contribute the active participation that rightly belongs to it. . . .
>
> 121. Composers, filled with the Christian spirit, should feel that their vocation is to develop sacred music and to increase its store of treasures.
>
> Let them produce compositions having the qualities proper to genuine sacred music, not confining themselves to works that can be sung only by

large choirs, but providing also for the needs of small choirs and for the active participation of the entire assembly of the faithful.

Article 114 cannot be read as a conciliar repudiation of the choir's function in Roman Rite worship; the statement that choirs are to be encouraged especially in cathedral churches does not restrict their use to the Ordinary's primary church building. The force of the document is to ensure that the choir never usurp the congregation's liturgical role, not that choirs be disbanded. Indeed the Council's exhortation to composers in article 120 strongly affirms the continued existence of choirs in Roman Rite worship, even though the personnel may take configurations other than the standard SATB divisions.

Much as SC notes in chapter one that promotion of the liturgical reform and renewal demands trained ministerial leadership, and therefore decrees that courses in liturgy be given to those in seminary and vowed life formation as well as active clergy and religious, so it decrees in chapter six that worship music education and formation must be a part of the programs preparing church leaders. The reference to young boys as liturgical singers is a nod to the boy choir tradition stemming from the understanding of the musical choir as a quasi-clerical entity:

> 115. Great importance is to be attached to the teaching and practice of music in seminaries, in the novitiates and houses of study of religious of both sexes, and also in other Catholic institutions and schools. To impart this instruction, those in charge of teaching sacred music are to receive thorough training.
>
> It is recommended that higher institutes of sacred music be established whenever possible.
>
> Musicians and singers, especially young boys, must also be given a genuine liturgical training.

Musicam Sacram

Parallel to Inst1958 as an implementation document for the papal teaching contained in MSD, MS as an implementation document for the conciliar teaching in SC begins by clarifying the fundamental categories of the baptized faithful engaged in Roman Catholic liturgical worship:

> 13. Liturgical services are celebrations of the Church, that is, of the holy people united in proper order under a bishop or priest. In a liturgical service the priest and his ministers have a special place because of holy orders; the servers, reader, commentator, and choir members because of the ministry they perform.

Compared with Inst1958, a radical simplification in conceptualization has occurred in MS. The primary subject of liturgical action is the gathered assembly of the baptized. Certain members of the faithful (bishops, presbyters, and deacons) are called to liturgical leadership by virtue of their ordination. Other members of the faithful have particular liturgical ministries to fulfill. But individual ministries arise from and return to the fundamental liturgical ministry of the assembly itself. Thus talk of direct but delegated and of authentic but indirect liturgical participation disappears from official Roman Rite documentation. A practical consequence of this understanding of liturgical ministry soon appears when the minor orders become reconceptualized as instituted ministries open to clerics and non-clerics alike in the 1968 *editio typica* of the ordination rites.

Much like Inst1958, MS notes the presidential role of presbyters and bishops in Roman Rite worship, a role that has a distinct musical responsibility:

> 14. Acting in the person of Christ, the priest presides over the gathered assembly. The prayers he sings or recites aloud are spoken in the name of the entire people of God and of all in the assembly; therefore all present must listen to them with reverence.

It is somewhat surprising that no mention is made of the deacon's liturgical ministry and its musical dimensions, since cantillating the gospel, leading litanies, cuing the assembly, and chanting the Exsultet have all traditionally been diaconal responsibilities.

The three forms of liturgical participation open to the baptized according to Inst1958 (internal, external, sacramental) are reiterated in MS (for sacramental participation see the remarks in 23c below), but a new greater emphasis on the need for silent participation appears in the latter document:

> 15. The faithful carry out their proper liturgical function by offering their complete, conscious, and active participation. The very nature of the liturgy demands this and it is the right and duty of the Christian people by reason of their baptism.
>
> This participation must be:
>
> a. internal, that is, the faithful make their thoughts match what they say and hear, and cooperate with divine grace;
>
> b. but also external, that is, they express their inner participation through their gestures, outward bearing, acclamations, responses, and song.
>
> The faithful are also to be taught that they should try to raise their mind to God through interior participation as they listen to the singing of ministers or choir.

16. A liturgical celebration can have no more solemn or pleasing feature than the whole assembly's expressing its faith and devotion in song. Thus an active participation that is manifested by singing should be carefully fostered along these lines:

a. It should include especially the acclamations, responses to the greetings of the priest and the ministers and responses in litanies, the antiphons and psalms, the verses of the responsorial psalm, and other similar verses, hymns and canticles.

b. Pertinent catechesis as well as actual practice should lead the people gradually to a more extensive and indeed complete participation in all the parts proper to them. . . .

18. At the proper times a holy silence is also to be observed. That does not mean treating the faithful as outsiders or mute onlookers at the liturgical service; it means rather making use of their own sentiments to bring them closer to the mystery being celebrated. Such sentiments are evoked by the word of God, the songs and the prayers, and the people's spiritual bond with the priest as he recites the parts belonging to the celebrant.

The majority of MS's treatment of worship music leadership is directed to the personnel, role, responsibilities, and architectural setting of choirs, as well as the technical and spiritual formation of individual choir members:

19. Because of the liturgical ministry it exercises, the choir *(capella musica; schola cantorum)* should be mentioned here explicitly.

The conciliar norms regarding reform of the liturgy have given the choir's function greater prominence and importance. The choir is responsible for the correct performance of the parts that belong to it, according to the differing types of liturgical assembly and for helping the faithful to take an active part in the singing.

Therefore:

a. Choirs are to be developed with great care, especially in cathedrals and other major churches, in seminaries, and in religious houses of study.

b. In smaller churches as well a choir should be formed, even if there are only a few members.

20. Over the centuries the choirs of basilicas, cathedrals, monasteries, and other major churches have won high praise because they have preserved and developed the priceless treasury of sacred music. By means of rules issued specifically for them and reviewed and approved by the Ordinary such choirs are to be continued in order to carry out liturgical celebrations with greater solemnity. . . .

22. Depending on the established customs of peoples and on other circumstances, a choir may be made up of men and boys, of all men or all boys, of both men and women, and, where the situation really requires, even of all women.

23. According to the design of the particular church, the place for the choir is to be such that:

a. its status as a part of the community with a special function is clearly evident;

b. the performance of its liturgical ministry is facilitated;

c. full, that is, sacramental, participation in the Mass remains convenient for each of the members.

When there are women members, the choir's place is to be outside the sanctuary.

24. In addition to musical training, choir members should receive instruction on the liturgy and on spirituality. Then the results of the proper fulfillment of their musical ministry will be the dignity of the liturgical service and an example for the faithful, as well as the spiritual benefit of the choir members themselves.

Most of this teaching simply repeats positions taken in Inst1958, but new criteria to determine the architectural placement of the choir appear. Since MS no longer conceptualizes the musical choir as a quasi-clerical entity, it is surprising that article 23c still directs that the placement of liturgical choirs with female members is to be outside the sanctuary.

Although neither SC nor MS oppose the roles of assembly and choir in musical worship, the following statements caution that the desire to sustain an earlier choral repertoire may never overwhelm the congregation's legitimate right to sing its faith:

[17] c. Some of the congregational parts may be assigned to the choir alone, however, especially when the people are not yet sufficiently trained or melodies for part-singing are used. But the people are not to be excluded from the other parts proper to them. The practice of assigning the singing of the entire Proper and Ordinary of the Mass to the choir alone without the rest of the congregation is not to be permitted. . . .

[20] Nevertheless choir directors and parish priests (pastors) or rectors of churches are to ensure that the congregation always joins in the singing of at least the more simple parts belonging to them.

The practical consequence of these articles is that the so-called Mass suite of the Renaissance, Baroque, Classical, Romantic, and early modern periods consisting of Kyrie, Gloria, Credo, Sanctus-Benedictus, and Agnus Dei could never be sung in its entirety during the renewed eucharistic liturgy since the vocal participation of the assembly is demanded at the "Profession of Faith" and "Holy, Holy, Holy," and presumed in the "Lord Have Mercy" and "Lamb of God." (According to the GIRM, the "Glory to God" could be sung by the choir alone without congregational vocal participation.)[1]

In contrast to the lengthy treatment of the liturgical choir, MS has only a few comments on the role of the cantor:

> 21. Especially when even a small choir is not possible, there must be at least one or more cantors, thoroughly trained to intone at least the simpler chants that the congregation sings and to lead and sustain the singing.
>
> Even in churches having a choir it is better for a cantor to be present for those celebrations that the choir cannot attend but that should be carried out with some degree of solemnity and thus with singing.

This article opens the door to a reconceptualization of the cantor's role in Roman Rite worship from a simple member of the *schola cantorum* responsible for intoning chants and leading litanies to an animator of the assembly's musical prayer. It is clear, however, that MS conceives of the cantor as a last resort substitute for a choir, which is the preferred form of musical leadership.

Finally, MS addresses composers and translators in its discussion of the process of generating vernacular Roman Rite liturgical music:

> 54. Translators of texts to be set to music should take care to combine properly conformity to the Latin and adaptability to the music. They are to respect the idiom and grammar of the vernacular and the proper characteristics of the people. Composers of new melodies are to pay careful heed to similar guidelines, as well as the laws of sacred music. . . .
>
> 56. Of special importance among the melodies to be composed for vernacular texts are those that belong to the priest and ministers for singing alone, together with the congregation, or in dialogue with the congregation. Composers of these melodies are to study whether the corresponding traditional melodies of the Latin liturgy may suggest melodies for use with the same texts in the vernacular. . . .
>
> 59. In their approach to a new work, composers should have as their motive the continuation of the tradition that provided the Church a genuine treasury of music for use in divine worship. They should thoroughly study the works of the past, their styles and characteristics; at the same time they should reflect on the new laws and requirements of the liturgy. The objective is that "any new form adopted should in some way grow organically from forms already existing" [SC 23] and that new works will become a truly worthy part of the Church's musical heritage.

These guidelines do not yet address authors as creators of new liturgical texts (i.e., those producing new vernacular texts for Roman Rite worship), but rather translators of the officially promulgated Latin texts.

Unlike Inst1958, MS does not specify the liturgical, linguistic, and musical training needed by composers, but contents itself to exhort them to produce compositions having organic ties to the earlier treasury of sacred music. Some composers have interpreted this to mean that they should continue composing in the styles of earlier eras (much as the "Caecilian" composers chose to compose in the style of Palestrina), while others have emulated not the styles of earlier Church composition but the pattern of engagement with one's culture represented by earlier composers.

Music in Catholic Worship

In applying the prescriptions of SC and MS to the United States, MCW discusses the various categories of Roman Rite worship music personnel that the earlier documents treated while revealing new emphases. It does not employ the fourfold categorization (ordained presiders, clerics, male substitutes for clerics, the rest of the baptized) appearing in Inst1958 or that used in MS (ordained liturgical ministers, unordained liturgical ministers, assembly). Rather, it grounds the discussion of all liturgical ministries in the activity of the assembly itself.

The worshiping assembly (termed "congregation" by MCW) captures the document's fullest attention. In contrast to the Roman documents, MCW highlights the diversity present within particular worshiping assemblies and indicates some consequences for its musical prayer. This insight into the pluralist character of many U.S. congregations will be developed and refined in later documents:

> 15. "The pastoral effectiveness of a celebration will be heightened if the texts of readings, prayers, and songs correspond as closely as possible to the needs, religious dispositions, and aptitude of the participants." [GIRM 313.] . . . The music used should be within the competence of most of the worshipers. It should suit their age-level, cultural background, and level of faith.

> 17. The diversity of people present at a parish liturgy gives rise to a further problem [in addition to that of "variations in the level of faith" treated in article 16]. Can the same parish liturgy be an authentic expression for a grade school girl, her college-age brother, their married sister with her young family, their parents and grandparents? Can it satisfy the theologically and musically educated along with those lacking in training? Can it please those who seek a more informal style of celebration? . . . Each Christian must keep in mind that to live and worship in community often demands a personal sacrifice. All must be willing to share likes and dislikes with others whose ideas and experiences may be quite unlike their own.

> 34. Music for the congregation must be within its members' performance capability. The congregation must be comfortable and secure with what they are doing in order to celebrate well.

While MCW underlines that Roman Rite worship must express the diversity of the worshipers, it may be insufficiently attentive to the power of the ritual and its music to create unity amidst diversity, the liturgy's unifying potential.

MCW treats the musical activity of the ordained in the context of other values for liturgical presidency:

> 21. No single factor affects the liturgy as much as the attitude, style, and bearing of the celebrant: his sincere faith and warmth as he welcomes the worshipping community; his human naturalness combined with dignity and seriousness as he breaks the Bread of Word and Eucharist.
>
> 22. The style and pattern of song ought to increase the effectiveness of a good celebrant. His role is enhanced when he is capable of rendering some of his parts in song, and he should be encouraged to do so. What he cannot sing well and effectively he ought to recite. If capable of singing, he ought, for the sake of the people, to rehearse carefully the sung parts that contribute to their celebration. [*Musicam Sacram* 8]

In speaking of the liturgical ministry of the ordained, MCW abandons the language of valid and licet celebration (categories ultimately derived from sacramental ontology) and substitutes the language of existential authenticity (categories ultimately derived from philosophical psychology). This emphasis on the human attractiveness of the ordained presider is a welcome corrective to rubrically correct but emotionally forbidding celebrants. Unfortunately, given the models for public discourse broadcast by the mass media in the United States, the focus on the presider's gifts may develop into an idiosyncratic attempt to entertain in the celebrant and a cult of personality on the part of the worshipers.

MCW clearly abandons the earlier distinctions between the *missa lecta* and the *missa cantata* based on the speaking or singing of the ordained presider. In the former discipline, the priest or bishop celebrant assigned to the sung Mass had to execute the prescribed chants whether or not he was capable of singing them accurately or in an edifying manner. With the disappearance of this discipline, presidential chanting has become the celebrant's choice, with two opposed consequences in pastoral practice: either the presidential texts are never chanted because the ordained presider feels uncomfortable singing alone in public or the presidential texts are crooned rather than cantillated.

MCW does not explicitly treat the worship music responsibilities of deacons in the Roman Rite.

Quoting the appropriate article from a 1966 instruction from the United States Bishops' Committee on the Liturgy [hereafter BCL], MCW stresses the role of the cantor in the renewed liturgy:

> 35. While there is no place in the liturgy for display of virtuosity for its own sake, artistry is valued, and an individual singer can effectively lead the assembly, attractively proclaim the Word of God in the psalm sung between the readings, and take his or her part in other responsorial singing. . . . Although a cantor "cannot enhance the service of worship in the same way as a choir, a trained and competent cantor can perform an important ministry by leading the congregation in common sacred song and in responsorial singing." [BCL Newsletter, 18 April 1966.]

MCW lists three functions for the cantor: leading the assembly's song, proclaiming God's word, and engaging responsorial singing. Presumably the first function would take place only in settings in which the congregation sings a capella, since the accompanying instrument(s) has the responsibility to support and lead the assembly's sung worship. In practice this function transfers the cantor's responsibility to intone chants from the *schola cantorum* to the assembly itself. The second function is properly artistic; the cantor does not simply intone the assembly's music, but makes an individual contribution to interpreting Scripture. Just as the non-gospel proclamations have their own ministers (lectors) and gospel proclamations have theirs (deacons preferably, but in their absence presbyters or bishops), so the proclamation of psalms and canticles involves its own proper minister, the cantor. The third function is more than simple intonation but less than an artistic interpretation of a liturgical text. Here the cantor provokes a sung response from the assembly (e.g., by chanting the invocations of a litany for the congregation's invariant refrain).

Note that MCW distinguishes the functions performed by choir and cantor. Unlike MS, MCW does not treat the cantor as a last resort substitute for the choir. Note as well that MCW does not demand that only males function as cantors, suggesting that it does not conceptualize the role as a quasi-clerical order, but after the model of the congregational director of song mentioned in Inst1958 96a.

In contrast to MS, MCW devotes relatively little attention to the role of the choir in renewed Roman Rite worship:

> 36. A well-trained choir adds beauty and solemnity to the liturgy and also assists and encourages the singing of the congregation. . . .

Apparently the document sees only two functions for the choir in the renewed Roman Rite liturgy: embellishing the ceremonial and supporting congregational singing. SS will strongly critique MCW for its lack of theoretical grounding for the choir's activity in the renewed Roman Rite liturgy (see below).

Finally, it should be noted that MCW makes no references to the roles of composers, authors, or commentators in its listing of the people responsible for Roman Rite worship music. Although it claims to treat the organist and instrumentalists in articles 37–38, these sentences really speak about the instruments played rather than the people playing them (and therefore will be treated in the following chapter).

Liturgical Music Today

LMT follows MCW's lead in grounding all individual worship music activity for the Roman Rite in that of the assembly:

> 63. The entire worshiping assembly exercises a ministry of music. Some members of the community, however, are recognized for the special gifts they exhibit in leading the musical praise and thanksgiving of Christian assemblies. These are the pastoral musicians, whose ministry is especially cherished by the Church.

This article confirms changes in terminology of some significance. First, it refers to a ministry of music. While SC spoke of the *munus ministeriale* exercised by liturgical music, neither it nor MS identified the worship music activity of the faithful, choirs, cantors, or instrumentalists as ministry; in fact, most official post-Vatican II Roman documents tend to restrict the term ministry to the ordained (bishops, presbyters, deacons) or the installed (lectors, acolytes). Second, LMT creates a new term and category for those who exercise worship music leadership in whatever format for Roman Rite worship: pastoral musicians. However differently gifted and trained composers, text-writers/translators, choir masters, community music directors, cantors, choir members, and instrumentalists may be, they all share a common vocation to shepherd (the root meaning of the term pastor) the sung prayer of the people of God at worship.

LMT recognizes the special role the ordained play in facilitating the assembly's sung prayer:

> 67. As the assembly's principal liturgical leaders, priests and deacons must continue to be mindful of their own musical role in the liturgy. Priests should grow more familiar with chanting the presidential prayers of the Mass and other rites. Deacons, too, in the admonitions, exhortations, and especially in the litanies of the third penitential rite and in the general intercessions of the Mass, have a significant musical role to play in worship.

For the first time, the worship music role of the deacon is explicitly acknowledged and specified.

LMT confirms and develops the new impetus given to the role of cantor in the reformed Roman Rite:

> 68. Among music ministers, the cantor has come to be recognized as having a crucial role in the development of congregational singing. Besides being qualified to lead singing, he or she must have the skills to introduce and teach new music, and to encourage the assembly. This must be done with sensitivity so that the cantor does not intrude on the communal prayer or become manipulative. Introductions and announcements should be brief and avoid a homiletic style.

> 69. The cantor's role is distinct from that of the psalmist, whose ministry is the singing of the verses of the responsorial psalm and communion psalm. Frequently the two roles will be combined in one person.

In addition to the roles of leading the assembly's song, proclaiming God's word, and engaging responsorial singing articulated by MCW, LMT envisions the cantor as an instructor for the assembly. This instruction involves both the direct teaching of music needed for liturgical celebration (although the document does not indicate when such teaching should take place) and various introductions and announcements, presumably taking place during the liturgy. Article 69 attempts to distinguish the role of psalmist from that of cantor, with the former a minister of the (sung) word of God and the latter a congregational facilitator. Such a distinction, though not conceptualized in the same way, can be found in earlier eras.[2] The distinction remains problematic, however. Not only has this distinction of roles been ignored in the vast majority of celebrations in the United States, the suggestion that the psalmist's proper texts are the responsorial psalm and the communion psalm raises questions of ritual function. The responsorial psalm appears as a wedding of text and music sung for its own sake as a proclamation alongside other scriptural proclamations in the Liturgy of the Word, while the communion psalm is a wedding of text and music sung to accompany congregational motion. It is difficult to see why singing the communion psalm should be the prerogative of the psalmist when the entrance psalm and preparation of the gifts psalm are equally processional in character.

Finally, in contrast to the development of the cantor's role in LMT, the document has little to say about the choir, the organist, or other instrumentalists.

The Milwaukee Report

Presuming the treatment of Roman Rite worship music personnel contained in SC, MS, MCW, and LMT, MR provides new terminology by which to identify and evaluate what LMT termed pastoral musicians, "musical leadership":

> 64. . . . Some have suggested that of all the elements influencing the musical participation of the assembly, the role of the musical leadership is the most determinative. Whether this assessment is true or not, the quality and character of the musical leadership has a major influence on the sung prayer of the assembly and on the entire celebration. We read in MCW: "Good celebrations foster and nourish faith. Poor celebrations may weaken and destroy it." Given the importance of musical leadership in affecting the quality of the celebration, one can conclude that "good musical leadership fosters and nourishes faith; poor musical leadership weakens and destroys it."

Having signaled the importance of all forms of musical leadership to Roman Rite worship, MR lists musical competence and pastoral sensitivity as the two fundamental qualities needed by all musical leaders:

> 65. Determining what is "good musical leadership" requires a culturally determined judgment. What might be good or appropriate musical leadership in one community, or with one kind of music, or in one cultural context, might not translate well into another. However, certain principles would seem to undergird effective and appropriate pastoral-musical leadership in any situation. One of this is musical competency. Music leaders must be skilled, artistically competent and secure in the exercise of their art. This is essential if the community is to be led ably in their song. Musical competency includes the ability to elicit a response from the assembly. A community is unable to join in the song when the musical demands far exceed the assembly's ability. A community is sometimes unwilling to join in when the quality of musical production so exceeds their own capacity that the only option is to listen. Music ministers need to draw on all of their professional, musical-liturgical skills in order to call forth the song of the assembly, which enjoys a definite preeminence in worship.

> 66. The effect of musically unskilled leadership is often easy to identify. Musical uncertainty in a vocalist or instrumentalist evokes similar insecurity and uncertainty in the assembly. Halting musical leadership can effectively destroy the song of the community. Musical competency is essential in order to avoid this dilemma. Sometimes more difficult is gauging the potential ill effects of over-performance on the part of the musical leadership in worship. In some respects this is a result of the pervasive influence of television in United States culture and the promotion of the entertainment model as the primary mode of public discourse in our society. We are used to performers who dazzle us with their talent. There is sometimes the expectation on the part of the assembly that worship will provide the same experiences. Musical leadership cast in the en-

tertainment mode transforms an assembly into an audience and believers into liturgical consumers. Music ministers need to examine their assumed model of musical leadership, to ensure that they habitually draw the assembly into the center of worship.

Strongly supporting the initiatives arising from MCW and LMT to conceptualize musical leadership as a genuine (if not formally recognized) liturgical ministry, MR underscores the need for pastoral musicians to embrace a life of Christian discipleship. This indirectly raises once again the theoretical concern about the ecclesial status of those engaged in musical leadership: should catechumens, members of other Christian ecclesial bodies, non-Christians or nonbelievers serve as composers, authors, choir masters, community music directors, choir members, cantors, and/or instrumentalists in Roman Rite worship?

> 72. Those who assume musical leadership in worship need to balance their skills with an awareness that their musicianship is always at the service of the assembly. There is no doubt that Christian liturgy benefits from the presence of skilled musicians even as it calls forth from them a new and necessary discipline. This discipline, seldom taught in our universities or conservatories, puts musicianship in an auxiliary role, handmaid to the liturgy. As noted in LMT, church musicians are called to be disciples first and then ministers. Our society may provide a variety of models for musicians, but many are devised for entertainment and are not appropriate for the liturgy. The nature of the liturgy requires a unique style of musical leadership: one that is, at its core, both professional and pastoral.

The Snowbird Statement

SS presents no comprehensive taxonomy of the people engaged in Roman Rite worship music; presumably, like MR, it accepts the frameworks presented in MS, MCW, and LMT. The closest it comes to such a listing appears in its discussion of the musical forms in the Church's liturgy:

> We wish to affirm standards of excellence in the composition and performance of all musical forms in the church's liturgy: congregational, choral, cantorial, diaconal, presidential and instrumental.

This catalog of musical forms is organized on the basis of personnel who execute the music rather than on the basis of literary genre (e.g., acclamations), ritual event (e.g., processionals), or musical characteristics (e.g., monody vs. polyphony; a capella vs. instrumentally accompanied). The bulk of the document's attention falls on the clergy's and the choir's musical leadership at Roman Rite worship, although it also suggests some strategies to form singing assemblies. It does not treat the role of the cantor. Taking its cue from Inst1958, SS asserts a need for professional musicians in Roman Rite worship and asserts the need for education and formation for all pastoral musicians.

SS expands MCW 22's declaration on the importance of the liturgical celebrant to include the musical responsibilities of all the clergy. It bewails the inadequacy of most ministerial formation programs' preparation for liturgical/musical leadership (in spite of directives from SC) through Roman congregations' guidelines for seminaries to the various editions of the United States bishops' *Program of Priestly Formation*:

> 12. The leadership of the parish clergy is the single most influential factor in the liturgical-musical life of the church; yet the formation of most seminarians in this area remains seriously inadequate. . . . Seminary formation requires a well-developed liturgical-musical curriculum which will allow future pastors to be good leaders in the worship life of their parishes and communities. Ongoing education for the clergy after seminary also needs to be more adequately organized within dioceses and religious communities.

SS strongly underlines SC's and MS's teaching on the need to maintain and develop choral singing in the Roman Rite. One of the document's most distinctive contributions is a call for deeper theoretical reflection on the role of the choir in Roman Rite worship, a forthright call that can be read as covert criticism of the relative neglect of the choir's ministry in MCW, LMT, and MR:

> 20. We are strongly committed to the renewal of the role of the choir in Catholic worship. There is nothing in the church's official directives since the Second Vatican Council that would justify the deprecation or elimination of the choir. . . . The voice of the choir and that of the congregation properly exist in dynamic relationship; there is no intrinsic conflict between the two. As part of the assembly, the choir at times leads congregational singing; at times it simply joins with the congregation; and at times it sings alone for the congregation's edification or to allow a ritual to unfold more expressively. It should not be forgotten that active participation on the part of the people is ensured both through actual singing and engaged listening. In no case should the choir offend against the proper norms for congregational singing. In all situations, a careful balance between the choir and congregation needs to be fostered.
>
> Deeper theological reflection on the nature of the liturgical choir is necessary in the Western church. Some, unfortunately, would reduce the choir's role exclusively to supporting and leading the assembly's song; many seem insufficiently aware of the ability of fine choral music to enhance worship. The resources for a more intensive exploration of the choir's role

in worship may be found in a closer examination of the structures of the liturgical rites, in the resources of Eastern liturgiology and aesthetics, as well as in modern theories of symbol and art. Such theoretical exploration of the role of the choir might well consider the following: the choir serves in a particular way to give voice to the glory and beauty of the liturgy; the choir bears witness to the eschatological fulfillment of the church, the song of which prefigures that of the saints and angelic choirs in the New Jerusalem; the choir is a joyful attendant of the pilgrim people of God and a festive sign of their heavenly home; the participation of the choir is crucial to the realization of solemnity and majesty in liturgical events.

In addition to its treatment of clerical and choral musical leadership in Roman Rite worship, SS also reflects on the assembly, evidencing a less-than-sanguine estimation of the practice of congregational singing more than three decades after SC was promulgated:

> 9. Central to the church's musical education programs must be the continued development of the singing congregation as the principal and fundamental musical body. Congregational singing in Catholic worship has not yet generally achieved a desirable standard. While no shortcuts or easy solutions exist, pastors and musicians would do well to reflect together more systematically and regularly on this matter and to choose and promote repertoire in a manner conducive to increased congregational singing. Catholic musical life in this area might benefit from detailed study of successful patterns in other Christian churches. . . .

> 11. The Catholic church's rich legacy of musical education of children and youth, extending back to early medieval times, needs to be rediscovered and promoted today. The musical formation of the young is critically important to the life of the church. . . . Success in this area may not be immediate, but it will be seen and heard in the liturgy of the future. From the ranks of children's choirs and music programs, where love for both the arts and for participation in the liturgy is fostered, future musicians will come forth to serve the church and its worship.

Note that the document suggests three strategies to develop better singing congregations. First, it calls for discernment in repertoire, presumably so that a common core of Christian ritual music might be identified in parish, diocese, and nation and so that idiosyncratic isolation of worshiping communities might be avoided. Second, somewhat surprisingly for a document that lauds a distinctively Catholic ethos of liturgical music, it suggests that Catholics turn to other unspecified Christian worshiping bodies to find models to encourage congregational singing. Third, it counsels developing children's and youth choirs, both to support the assembly's song and enhance the ceremony of community worship and to develop future assembly singers. Note that unlike the earlier Roman documents' emphasis on

boys' choirs, SS envisions musical formation of young males and females alike.

Inst1958, while showing preference for musical leaders who
would offer their services to the Church without seeking monetary remuneration, acknowledged that some musicians might actually be
employed by the Church for the sake of its worship music. SS strongly
defends the role of the professional church musician:

> 15. We affirm the value to the church of trained, full-time professional mu-
> sicians. Though such musicians will always constitute a minority in the
> service of the church, their expertise and influence are a crucial resource
> for the broader development of the church's liturgical life. By their ex-
> ample, collaboration and sharing of talents, such musicians assist and sup-
> port other lesser-trained or part-time musicians in parishes and smaller
> communities. No conceptual or practical opposition need exist between
> the full-time professional and the part-time volunteer. In an increasingly
> professionalized ecclesiastical environment, wherein the majority of those
> involved are lay people, it is surprising to see a professional role of long
> standing—the full-time church musician—being regarded by some today
> as obsolete or an affront to the common call to service.

Thus SS seems to reverse Inst1958's preference for volunteer musical
leadership. While there are undoubted benefits to the service a full-
time music professional may offer Roman Rite worship, one may question the application of a professional model to church ministry,
especially in a Roman Catholic context.[3]

Finally, SS highlights the need for on-going education and formation for leaders in all branches of service to the Church's musical
prayer:

> 10. We call for more adequate resources to improve the musical skills of
> parish musicians of all level of competence. There exists a serious need
> for moral and financial support in this area from parishes, dioceses and
> episcopal conferences. The most important skill of the parish musician,
> apart from adequate understanding of the liturgy, is the actual ability to
> make music. When this is lacking, the song of the assembly cannot be ac-
> tualized and the rites cannot be celebrated adequately. Basic musical
> skills to be fostered include, for example, keyboard playing which en-
> courages congregational singing and vocal technique which enables
> proclamation of a psalm verse. We envision graded listings of necessary
> musical skills articulated by the national episcopal conference or by
> diocesan music offices. We regard the fostering of musical competence in
> liturgical musicians as a primary task of the diocesan music director and
> the obligation of every bishop.

In this chapter we have traced changes in the understanding of the appropriate people who are to make Roman Rite worship music.

In the initial documents the responsibility devolved upon clerics: the ordained by virtue of their liturgical presidency cantillated the prescribed chants and the clerical choir performed more complex music. When a clerical choir could not be organized, a musical choir consisting of men and/or boys could substitute; not only were these singers to execute the compositions well, their lives were to serve as moral exemplars to the rest of the faithful. Cantors at this time functioned only to intone the choral chants and to lead litanies. The faithful were encouraged to assist the clerical choir in singing according to their capacity, but women, being incapable of a priestly office, could not be members of a liturgical choir.

Later pre-Vatican II documents modify these perceptions and prescriptions. The clergy are still expected to cantillate the prescribed chants. As the musical choir ceased to be conceptualized as a substitute for the clerical choir, women and girls were gradually admitted. The responsibilities and formation of composers, authors, organists/choir directors, singers, and instrumentalists were all addressed. The role of commentator appeared as a quasi-clerical entity and women were forbidden to occupy this role; they could, however, serve as directors of congregational song and leaders of the assembly's (vernacular) prayer.

SC and its implementation document, MS, emphasize the full, conscious, and active participation of the baptized faithful by means of music in Roman Rite liturgy. The presiding clergy and choir continue to play leadership roles. The cantor is given a new role: from being the member of the *schola cantorum* who intones the prescribed chants to serving as a choir substitute.

Official and scholarly documents in the United States underscore the priority placed on the assembly's song. Gradually musical responsibilities are clarified both for priests (i.e., bishops and presbyters) and deacons. After a short period of relative neglect, the role of the choir gains greater theoretical justification; in pastoral practice the standard SATB choral group is supplemented by a variety of vocal/instrumental ensembles. The greatest development occurs in the role of the cantor, which moves from being considered a choir substitute to an animator of the assembly's song, an artistic interpreter of God's word, a community music teacher, and an instrument of ritual flow. The role of the commentator, in contrast, disappears. Roles for both professional and volunteer music ministers or pastoral musicians continue to develop after the Council.

Now that we have gained some sense of the people who are intended to make Roman Catholic worship music according to the documents under examination, we turn to an investigation of the musical instruments by which such worship music might be performed.

ENDNOTES

[1] This interpretation is strongly supported later in the document:

"34. When there is to be part-singing for the chants of the Ordinary of the Mass, they may be sung by the choir along in the customary way, that is, either a cappella or with instrumental accompaniment. The Congregation, however, must not be altogether left out of the singing for the Mass.

"In other cases the chants of the Ordinary may be divided between choir and congregation or between one part of the congregation and another. The singing is then done by alternating verses or in any other way that takes in most of the entire text. It is important in any such arrangement, however, to attend to the following. Because it is a profession of faith, the *Credo* is best sung by all or else sung in a manner that allows the congregation's proper participation. Because it is an acclamation concluding the preface, the *Sanctus* should as a rule be sung by the entire assembly along with the priest. Because it accompanies the breaking of the bread, the *Agnus Dei* may be repeated as often as necessary, especially in concelebrations and it is appropriate as well for the congregation to have a part in it, at least by singing the final *Grant us peace*."

[2] For example, William Durand distinguishes between cantors (including three subcategories of precentor, succentor, and concentor) and psalmists in book II, chs. 2–3 of his monumental medieval liturgical commentary, the *Rationale divinorum officiorum.*

[3] "The concerns in recent years to assert that ministers are to be understood as professionals emerges in part from our sense that our status and function in society are no longer as clear or as prestigious as once they were. . . .

"It is also true that the turn to the model of professionalism has roots more honorable and perhaps more enduring than our injured pride. On the one hand, in freer Protestant churches, . . . questions of ordination remain murky. We have tended to deny that there is any qualitative difference between the call to ministry and any other call. We define the clergy therefore not ontologically, or sacramentally, but functionally. Clergy are those who are paid, hired, to perform particular jobs for the congregation. We are professionals, not professional Christians, but Christians whose profession is defined in relationship to the institutional church, which hires, pays, and sometimes lets us go.

"On the other hand, the attempt to understand the clergy as professionals emerges in part from the honorable attempt to understand the church in its present context, for our purposes, in twentieth-century North America. . . . In our time the two forms of leadership that have prevailed in the definition of ministry are the minister as manager (for the sake of the institution) and the minister as therapist (for the sake of the individual believer). . . .

"Yet what one senses in the shift to the professional model for ministry is an insufficient attention to our sources, to the foundational texts and experiences out of which the church emerged. . . . As we consider the question of ministers as professionals in our time we need . . . conversation with the gospel; more, we begin the search for our identity there." David L. Bartlett, *Ministry in the New Testament,* Overtures to Biblical Theology (Minneapolis: Fortress Press, 1993) 14–15.

5

What Instruments Are to Make Roman Catholic Worship Music?

Having explored how the nine documents we are studying identify Roman Catholic worship music, its purpose and functions, its qualities, and the persons who execute it, our final investigation considers the instruments deemed appropriate for Roman Catholic worship.

Tra le sollecitudini

While underscoring the logocentric character of Roman Rite worship music, TLS acknowledges that instrumental music may make its own contribution in accompanying sung prayer:

15. Although the proper music of the Church is only vocal, nevertheless the accompaniment of an organ is allowed. . . .

16. Since the singing must always be the chief thing, the organ and other instruments may only sustain and never crush it. . . .

The document simply acknowledges pastoral practice; it nowhere provides a theoretical justification for the use of purely instrumental music in Roman Rite worship.

TLS then categorizes particular instruments as appropriate and inappropriate for Roman Rite worship on the basis of their sacred or profane character:

18. The music of the organ in the accompaniment, preludes, interludes, and so on must be played not only according to the proper character of the instrument, but also according to all the rules of real sacred music, which have been described above.

19. The use of the pianoforte is forbidden in churches, as also that of all noisy or irreverent instruments, such as drums, kettledrums, cymbals, triangles and so on.

20. Bands are strictly forbidden to play in church, and only for some special reason, after the consent of the Bishop has been obtained, may a certain number of specially chosen wind instruments be allowed, which must be carefully selected and suitable to their object; and the music they play must always be reverent, appropriate, and in every way like that of the organ.

The pipe organ is clearly viewed as a sacred instrument; other wind instruments may be employed insofar as they approximate the organ's sound, thus emulating its sacredness. (This directive may strike the reader as somewhat peculiar since one of the characteristics of organ voicing and registration is the approximation of other wind, string, and percussion instruments' sounds by the organ pipes.) In contrast, the piano and various percussion instruments are forbidden in Roman Rite worship music, not because they are incapable of accompanying the assembly's song (the primary reason given in TLS for the use of the organ in Roman Rite worship), but because they are deemed noisy and irreverent, i.e., profane or secular. One might think that the qualities of noisiness and irreverence might describe the possible manner of *playing* instruments rather than a quality that inheres in particular instruments *in se*. (Ethnomusicological research indicates, however, that some cultures identify particular instruments as sacred and others as secular, but the evaluation is culturally coded, not a transcultural characteristic.) It is interesting to note that TLS mentions neither plucked nor bowed string instruments in its taxonomy (nor, of course, electronic instruments, which had yet to be developed).

Musicae sacrae disciplina

MSD advances the discussion of instruments in Roman Rite worship by providing additional criteria for determining appropriateness. Like TLS, MSD lauds the use of the organ:

58. Among the musical instruments that have a place in church, the organ rightly holds the principal position, since it is especially fitted for the sacred chants and sacred rites. It adds a wonderful splendor and a special magnificence to the ceremonies of the Church. It moves the souls of the faithful by the grandeur and sweetness of its tones. It gives minds an almost heavenly joy and it lifts them up powerfully to God and to higher things.

Instead of repeating TLS's justification for the use of the organ in accompanying singing, MSD adduces three other reasons. First, the variety of timbres and intensity of sound that the organ is capable of

producing can create an aura of sober festivity quite congruent with
Roman Rite liturgical worship. Second, the organ can evoke emotion
in its listeners; one could remark that this ability seems true for the
voice as well as for other musical instruments. Finally, MSD declares
that the organ can fulfill a transcendental function, intimating in its
sounds a realm of beauty beyond that of everyday life; again this characteristic does not seem unique to the organ.

Unlike TLS, MSD does not provide a taxonomy of forbidden instruments. Instead it offers three criteria to help discern appropriate
and inappropriate candidates:

> 59. Besides the organ, other instruments can be called upon to give great
> help in attaining the lofty purpose of sacred music, so long as they play
> nothing profane, nothing clamorous or strident and nothing at variance
> with the sacred services or the dignity of the place.

These criteria are somewhat problematic. First, clamorousness or stri-
dency characterizes particular compositions and/or the way in which
they are played rather than inhering in particular instruments. (These
raucous musical qualities might be functions of timbre, volume, and/or
rhythm). Second, while MSD demands that musical instruments play
only compositions congruent with Roman Rite religious services, the
criteria for determining such compositions remain underdeveloped.
Third, the document asserts that the instruments employed must produce a sound proportionate to the acoustic space; thus instruments
that could be quite appropriate for smaller gatherings and spaces may
be out of place in vast worship spaces.

Unlike TLS, which singled out wind instruments when played to
approximate an organ as appropriate instruments for Roman Rite worship, MSD lauds bowed string instruments:

> 59. . . . Among these [appropriate instruments] the violin and other mu-
> sical instruments that use the bow are outstanding because, when they
> are played by themselves or with other stringed instruments or with the
> organ, they express the joyous and sad sentiments of the soul with an in-
> describable power.

Note that bowed string instruments are applauded not for their ability
to accompany singing; rather, they are praised for their ability to evoke
emotion in listeners. This insight is problematic for two reasons: (1) as
noted above in our treatment of the organ, one might argue that other
plucked string, wind, percussion, and electronic instruments might
equally well evoke emotion; and (2) official and pastoral documents
usually deprecate strong emotional reactions during the course of
Roman Rite worship.

In an almost humorous aside MSD cautions that good will cannot replace musical competence in the playing of instruments at Roman Rite worship:

> 61. It should hardly be necessary to add the warning that, when the means and talent available are unequal to the task, it is better to forego such attempts than to do something which would be unworthy of divine worship and sacred gatherings.

The 1958 Instruction

Inst1958 returns to TLS's categorization of the instruments appropriate for Roman Rite worship on the basis of their status as sacred or profane, though the taxonomy of forbidden instruments changes. One presumes that absolute prohibition of piano and percussion instruments and the partial prohibition of wind ensembles articulated in TLS continues, with Inst1958 adding new examples of forbidden electronic instruments:

> 70. Those musical instruments which by common consent and usage are suited only for profane music must be absolutely prohibited in liturgical functions and pious exercises.
>
> 71. The use of "automatic" instruments and machines such as the automatic organ, phonograph, the radio, dictaphone, or tape recorder, and other similar devices, are absolutely forbidden in liturgical functions, or pious exercises, whether inside or outside the church, even if they are used only to transmit sacred discourses or music, or to replace or assist the singing of the choir or the faithful.

No reasons are given for the prohibition of these electronic instruments. What seems to categorize all of them, however, is their ability to create sound without the direct activity of a living human soundmaker. MSD seems to suggest that the authenticity of Roman Rite music demands that the musical participation of the faithful be generated by those actually present at a service, rather than by a prerecorded performance.

Nonetheless not all technological sound manipulation is forbidden:

> 72. "Loudspeakers" may be used in liturgical functions and pious exercises.

Although Inst1958 gives no reason for permitting the use of sound amplification devices in Roman Rite worship, they are probably allowed because, unlike the automatic instruments listed in article 71, they increase the volume (and change the timbre) of sounds produced by actual living participants. Later documents will note how the use of sound amplification devices has changed the acoustic environment of Roman Rite worship with rather significant consequences.

Although one might argue that these percussion instruments are used for signaling rather than musical purposes in Roman Rite worship, Inst1958 acknowledges and approves the use of bells:

> 88. The approved customs and the different way of ringing the bells, according to the various purposes for which they are rung, are to be carefully preserved. Ordinaries of places should set down the traditional and customary norms in this matter, or, if there are none, to prescribe them.

Presumably the document is referring to the hand bells used by acolytes or altar servers and the tower bells or carillon associated with worship spaces rather than the use of orchestra bells, concert handbells, or glockenspiel.

Sacrosanctum Concilium

SC both confirms and departs from earlier official teaching on the role of instruments in Roman Rite worship:

> 120. In the Latin Church the pipe organ is to be held in high esteem, for it is the traditional musical instrument that adds a wonderful splendor to the Church's ceremonies and powerfully lifts up the spirit to God and to higher things.

> But other musical instruments also may be admitted for use in divine worship, with the knowledge and consent of the competent territorial authority. . . . This applies, however, only on condition that the instruments are suitable, or can be made suitable, for sacred use, are in accord with the dignity of the place of worship, and truly contribute to the uplifting of the faithful.

On the one hand, in phrases adapted from MSD, SC affirms the role of the pipe organ in Roman Rite worship. Note that the document technically lauds the pipe organ rather than the harmonium, reed organ, or electronic instruments. The reference to the pipe organ as a traditional musical instrument in Roman Rite worship is somewhat misleading since in the patristic and early medieval eras organs were forbidden in Christian worship due to the raucousness of their tone. Even the organ's role in accompanying chant seems to be a nineteenth-century European development.[1] It is again surprising that MS does not recognize the organ's role in accompanying congregational song as did TLS. Also one wonders if the Council Fathers deliberately removed MSD's references to the organ's ability to evoke emotion.

On the other hand, SC no longer discusses the appropriateness of instruments for Roman Rite worship in terms of their ontology, but of their function. There is no taxonomy of permitted sacred instruments or forbidden profane instruments. Rather, any instrument may potentially appear in Roman Rite worship if it fulfills three criteria. First, in cultures that designate particular instruments for non-Christian cultic use, such instruments must be purified of any pagan worship connotations before they can be employed in Roman Rite worship. Second, echoing MSD, SC teaches that the sound production of the instrument must be congruent with the acoustic space in which it plays. Finally, SC acknowledges the cultural codes operative in the use of certain instruments and demands that those chosen must be capable of genuinely edifying worshipers, rather than entertaining or shocking them.

Musicam Sacram

In implementing the worship music decisions of SC for the Roman Rite, MS provides a more systematic treatment of the topic of instrumental music in Roman Rite worship than the earlier documents. Accompanying song and playing pure music provide the two foundational categories for MS's discussion of the topic:

> 62. Musical instruments either accompany the singing or played alone can add a great deal to liturgical celebrations.

The ordering of the explanatory articles suggests that accompanying sung ritual texts may be the more important function for instrumental music in Roman Rite worship:

> 64. Musical instruments as the accompaniment for singing have the power to support the voice, to facilitate participation, and to intensify the unity of the worshipping assembly. But their playing is not to drown out the voice so that the texts cannot be easily heard. Instruments are to be silent during any part sung by the priest or ministers by reason of their function.

> 65. As accompaniment for the choir or congregation the organ or other lawfully acceptable instruments may be played in both sung and read Masses.

But purely instrumental music also contributes to the liturgy's spiritual power:

> 65. . . . Solo playing is allowed at the beginning of Mass, prior to the priest's reaching the altar, at the presentation of the gifts, at the communion, and at the end of Mass. . . .

66. Solo playing of musical instruments is forbidden during Advent, Lent, the Easter triduum, and at services and Masses for the dead.

Article 65 does not restrict purely instrumental music solely to the moments of the eucharistic liturgy mentioned; rather it suggests two ritual functions for such music: (1) providing a musical framework to cover ritual activity (presentation of gifts, communion) and (2) providing a sonic environment to assist the worshipers' transition from/to the world outside the liturgy. By forbidding purely instrumental music during certain liturgical seasons, feasts, and celebrations, article 66 suggests that it is a mark of joyful festivity, inappropriate to more penitential or sorrowful occasions. One could argue that appropriate purely instrumental music might enhance penitential or sorrowful liturgical gatherings as well as joyous ones. Alternatively forbidding purely instrumental music on these occasions may actually serve as the aural equivalent of bodily fasting: the absence of such artistic embellishment during these periods may heighten its impact in other seasons or feasts.

Unlike TLS, MSD, and Inst1958, MS does not provide a taxonomy of permitted or forbidden instruments. Rather, like MSD and SC, the document provides criteria to discern appropriate and inappropriate instruments:

63. One criterion for accepting and using musical instruments is the genius and traditions of the particular peoples. At the same time, however, instruments that are generally associated and used only with worldly music are to be absolutely barred from liturgical services and religious devotions. All musical instruments accepted for divine worship must be played in such a way as to meet the requirements of any liturgical service and to contribute to the beauty of worship and the building up of the faithful.

Note that no claims are made about the ability to identify sacred and profane instruments per se. Rather, the cultural associations of particular instruments must be taken into account if they are to be introduced into Roman Rite worship. Other criteria simply repeat insights from MSD, Inst1958, and SC.

Modifying Inst1958's call for musical competence on the part of instrumentalists, MS adds a requirement that they be formed and educated in the meaning of the liturgy:

67. It is, of course, imperative that organists and other musicians be accomplished enough to play properly. But in addition they must have a deep and thorough knowledge of the significance of the liturgy. That is required in order that even their improvisations will truly enhance the

celebration in accord with the genuine character of each of its parts and will assist the participation of the faithful.

Music in Catholic Worship

In adapting the provisions of SC and MS to the United States, MCW does not advance the theoretical justification for the use of instruments in Roman Rite worship beyond the earlier documents:

> 37. Song is not the only kind of music suitable for liturgical celebration. Music performed on the organ and other instruments can stimulate feelings of joy and contemplation at appropriate times. [Cf. CSL 120; MS 63–65; Lect. Intro 3c.] This can be done effectively at the following points: an instrumental prelude, a soft background to a spoken psalm, at the preparation of the gifts in place of singing, during portions of the communion rite, and the recessional. . . .

In MCW's nonexhaustive listing of possible places for instrumental music, it provides a new category: the use of instrumental background music behind a spoken text. Such an expansion of the category sets up certain theoretical and practical problems. Technically this practice cannot be considered pure music since spoken language is involved. In addition, are there other spoken liturgical texts that might be enhanced by such a sonic background? If so, what are they? If not, why does the spoken (responsorial) psalm have this unique status? Culturally such a use of music may be associated with consumerism, advertising, and mass media presentations with possible problematic connections to Roman Rite worship.

Like the later Roman documents, MCW refrains from providing a taxonomy of permitted and forbidden instruments, preferring instead to sketch some criteria for discernment:

> 37. . . . In the dioceses of the United States, "musical instruments other than the organ may be used in liturgical services, provided they are played in a manner that is suitable to public worship." [NCCB, Nov. 1967; cf. CSL 120.] This decision deliberately refrains from singling out specific instruments. Their use depends on circumstances, the nature of the congregation, etc.

Liturgical Music Today

LMT advances the discussion of instrumental music in United States Roman Rite worship far beyond that of earlier documents. First it notes that both a capella singing and a variety of instrumental combinations accompanying singing are appropriate:

> 14. . . . In the same celebration music may be rendered in various ways: unaccompanied; or accompanied by organ, piano, guitar or other instruments.

Note that this article explicitly repudiates the teaching of TLS with reference to the use of the piano.

While acknowledging the logocentric character of Roman Rite worship music, LMT reasserts the two fundamental reasons justifying instrumental music adduced by MS:

> 56. The liturgy prefers song to instrumental music. . . . Yet the contribution of instrumentalists is also important, both in accompanying the singing and in playing by themselves.
>
> 57. Church music legislation of the past reflected a culture in which singing was not only primary, but was presumed to be unaccompanied (chant and polyphony). The music of today, as indeed musical culture today, regularly presumes that the song is accompanied. This places instruments in a different light. The song achieves much of its vitality from the rhythm and harmony of its accompaniment. Instrumental accompaniment is a great support to an assembly in learning new music and in giving full voice to its prayer and praise in worship.
>
> 58. Instrumental music can also assist the assembly in preparing for worship, in meditating on the mysteries, and in joyfully progressing in its passage from liturgy to life. Instrumental music, used in this way, must be understood as more than an easily dispensable adornment to the rites, a decoration to dress up a ceremony. It is rather ministerial, helping the assembly to rejoice, to weep, to be of one mind, to be converted, to pray. There is a large repertoire of organ music which has always been closely associated with the liturgy. Much suitable music can be selected from the repertoires of other appropriate instruments as well.

What is new in these articles is the further theoretical emancipation of instrumental music in Roman Rite worship. In addition to its functions of accompanying singing, covering ritual motion, providing a sonic transition into and out of the liturgical event, and providing background for spoken texts, LMT notes that instrumental music has an educational function as well, assisting the assembly to learn new music and to execute it with confidence. Like MSD, LMT underscores the ability of instrumental music to evoke emotion in worshipers, but unlike the earlier document, LMT does not restrict such a function to the organ or bowed string instruments.

As a possible corrective to MCW's embrace of instrumental music played as background to a spoken text, LMT cautions against the use of instrumental improvisations to submerge worship in a sea of ambient sound:

> 59. The proper place of silence must not be neglected, and the temptation must be resisted to cover every moment with music. [GIRM, 23; GILOTH 202; Part VI Apostolic Exhortation Evangelica Testificatro (29 June 1971),

46.] There are times when an instrumental interlude is able to bridge the gap between two parts of a ceremony and help to unify the liturgical action. But music's function is always ministerial and must never degenerate into idle background music.

Finally LMT, echoing the teaching in Inst1958, provides a justification for avoiding the use of prerecorded music in Roman Rite worship:

60. The liturgy is a complexus of signs expressed by living human beings. Music, being preeminent among those signs, ought to be "live." While recorded music, therefore, might be used to advantage outside the liturgy as an aid in the teaching of new music, it should, as a general norm, never be used within the liturgy to replace the congregation, the choir, the organist or other instrumentalists.

The Milwaukee Report

MR does not directly address the issue of appropriate instruments for Roman Rite worship, but in its discussion of "Technology and Worship" the document nuances the position taken in Inst1958 and LMT about the use of prerecorded music:

78. Great strides have been made over the past few decades in the sound reproduction of previously recorded music. The principle about prerecorded music, articulated in LMT, still holds true: "It should, as a general norm, never be used within the liturgy to replace the congregation, the choir, the organist or other instrumentalists." While prerecorded music should never replace the congregation and the other ministers of music within worship, prerecorded music can support the ritual engagement of these ministers, or musically supply a resource that may be lacking in a local community. Such technology enables communities to reproduce a repertoire and quality level seldom achievable on a local level. It is not only the considerations of expanded repertoire and superior musical quality, however, that are the criteria for deciding whether or not prerecorded music should be employed within worship. Rather, it is first and foremost whether the recording will enable or impede the community's participation.

MR's functionalist approach to Roman Rite worship music demands that prerecorded music not be blanketly condemned from an ontological perspective (as TLS had previously done with the piano and certain percussion instruments), as if prerecorded music were inherently profane. Rather, particular pieces of prerecorded music must be judged in the context of a particular worshiping assembly to determine whether or not they will genuinely enable the congregation to actively participate in musical worship. Presumably this discussion does not concern pieces of electronic music conceived for and executed by recording technology, as in the use of a tape recorded score coordinated with live organ and vocal performance. What seems to be envisaged are pastoral practices such as the playing of instrumental recordings during individual confessions in a communal penance service.

A different pastoral situation obtains with prerecorded accompaniments for live assemblies in isolated and/or economically deprived communities with few or no musical instrument resources:

> 79. Another technology that affects our worship is the digital memory available in numerous electronic instruments. This allows, for example, an organist to prerecord an accompaniment for a hymn, which can then be played back during worship with or without the presence of the accompanist. Like prerecording accompaniments to various hymns and other worship music currently available, this technology can appear to be a useful solution to the unavailability of competent liturgical musicians. While there are some pastoral situations where this technology will aid and enable the prayer and song of the people, there are also inherent difficulties. Accompanying a congregation is a dynamic, not a mechanical act. Removing the human equation from the act of liturgical accompaniment certainly diminishes the dynamic quality of that event. As a general norm, therefore, prerecorded or digitally recorded accompaniments should be avoided. *A capella* singing is to be preferred.

In conformity with its functionalist stance, MR does not condemn such technology outright but offers the prudential judgment that in fact a capella singing would more effectively enable communities' musical worship.

The Snowbird Statement

In contrast to MR's reticence about identifying particular instruments as appropriate or forbidden in Roman Rite worship, SS forthrightly champions the organ and critiques the use of instruments associated with what has been termed by some the "contemporary ensemble":

> 23. We underscore the value of the pipe organ as a most effective leader of congregational singing, especially in large assemblies. With its wide dynamic range, its variety of tonal color and especially its air-supported, sustained sound, the pipe organ offers a most effective support for congregational singing. The experimentation with guitars, pianos and other instruments over the past three decades has only proven the greater effectiveness of the organ. For smaller congregations and in small spaces, the use of other acoustical instruments such as the piano, guitar and wind instruments can be effective. These instruments need not be abandoned,

but their use as instruments of broad congregational support is clearly limited. We invite a more critical attitude to claims that electronic instruments are equally effective and economical, and we encourage the installation of even small pipe organs in situations where resources are limited.

SS returns to TLS's foundational justification for the use of the organ in Roman Rite worship as an accompaniment for singing, though the focus is now on the support that it can provide for the assembly's song rather than for that of the (quasi-)clerical choir. The contention that acoustical ensemble instruments are limited in their ability to sustain congregational singing is asserted rather than proven. It would perhaps be more accurate to suggest that all instruments have strengths and weaknesses for supporting a singing assembly: while the organ's ability to surround the congregation with sustained sound supports some forms of community singing, it is usually less successful in propelling syncopated rhythms in other forms. The quick decay of the piano's sound is generally less successful than the sustained tones of the organ in surrounding the congregation, but it may more powerfully project complex rhythms. Both keyboards may combine with a wide variety of other instruments, but the forms of interaction will typically be different. SS echoes SC in its preference for pipe organs over electronic instruments, but the reasons for such a preference remain underdeveloped assertions rather than warranted conclusions.

Like MR, SS is skeptical of the use of prerecorded music in Roman Rite music:

> 25. The use of recorded music is a great temptation in Catholic worship today, especially where adequate musical resources are lacking. This option, attractive as it may appear, should be discouraged as antithetical to the nature of the liturgy as the living act of God's people. Nothing should substitute for or impede the functioning of the assembly in actual liturgical celebrations. The use of recorded choirs, organs and cantors, though they can seem to serve an immediate need, has the effect of discouraging local communities from marshalling the resources necessary for the authentic celebration of the liturgy.

It is interesting that SS here joins MR in a functionalist critique of prerecorded music.

As in the other areas we have investigated, radical shifts in thought have occurred concerning the use of instruments in Roman Rite worship during the course of the twentieth century.

The earliest documents we have studied assert the properly logocentric character of Roman Rite worship music and can provide little theoretical justification for the use of instruments other than to accompany singing. Musical instruments are categorized as sacred or profane not on the basis of how they are culturally tagged or how they are played, but with reference to their being. On this basis taxonomies of permitted and forbidden instruments are constructed.

Later documents provide further reasons for the use of instruments in Roman Rite worship: evoking emotion, accompanying ritual motion, helping worshipers to bridge between their daily lives and the world of the liturgy, providing a sonic background for a spoken text, facilitating singers in learning new repertoire. Musical instruments are classified less as sacred or profane per se, but are conceived more functionally: in their ability to evoke the assembly's prayer, facilitate the liturgical ritual, accord with the acoustic space, and avoid anti-Christian connotations. Lists of permitted and forbidden instruments thus have to be developed by taking into account the cultural codes of the worshipers.

The most recent documents have drawn special attention to the impact of technology on the acoustic environment of Roman Rite worship. On the one hand, new technologies have vastly expanded the possibilities for sound enhancement and reproduction; on the other, such technologies may overwhelm rather than assist worshiping assemblies.

ENDNOTE

[1] See J. Bonfils, "Note historique sur le rôle de l'orgue dans la liturgie catholique," *L'Eglise qui chante* 16 (1959) 7–8.

Conclusion

This study of nine twentieth-century documents concerned with Roman Catholic worship music clearly identifies the revolution that has taken place both in theory and practice in this century. I conclude with a few thoughts about the future of Roman Rite worship music in the United States.

First, there is still much confusion over what constitutes proper liturgical music. After restrictions of language and style were removed by SC, Roman Rite Catholics have been exposed to worship music from an incredible variety of sources. Some of the compositions have exactly reproduced the officially approved vernacular translations of the reformed liturgical texts, others have paraphrased them, and still others have made no reference to these official texts at all. Roman Catholics have imported worship music generated for other Christian traditions into their worship: Orthodox chants, Anglican anthems, Lutheran, Methodist, and Baptist hymns, charismatic praise choruses, and camp meeting songs. Many communities have also employed compositions taken from secular sources, singing "Prepare Ye" from *Godspell* as an Advent processional, "Sunrise, Sunset" from *Fiddler on the Roof* for weddings, "From a Distance" for youth masses, etc. Distinctions between witness and testimony music, political rally and consciousness-raising songs, catechetical music and properly liturgical music continue to be blurred in practice. Much conversation and careful thought will be needed to sort out what genuinely supports and sustains Roman Rite vernacular worship and what properly belongs to other venues.

Second, in spite of the exhortations of SC and the post-Vatican II implementation documents, the treasury of sacred music consisting of Gregorian chant, Ars Nova and Renaissance polyphony, Baroque, Classical, and Romantic Masses, Requiems, and motets has almost completely disappeared from Rome Rite worship. Concentrated efforts must be engaged if elements of this repertoire are to be retained in Roman Rite worship as living prayer rather than museum curiosities.

Third, the impact of sound technology and the mass media on U.S. culture and worship must be more forthrightly addressed. A century ago if one wanted to experience music one either produced it oneself or went to an acoustic environment (back porch, concert hall, local church) where other living human beings produced it. With the invention of recording technology, live performances could be fixed in another medium for reproduction at a later date in the absence of live performers. But even then others could share in the listening experience because the reproduced sound filled a common acoustic environment. With the invention of personal sound systems such as the Sony Walkman, technology created a totally private acoustic environment with the direct implication that individuals should be able to "consume" music according to their personal tastes and preferences. When Roman Rite worship music prizes communal music making rather than music consumption, and when it calls for a submission of individual taste preferences to the common act of liturgical music making, it takes a fiercely countercultural stance.

Fourth, U.S. citizens live in an increasingly pluralist postmodern world. This is represented not only by the multiple languages and ethnic heritages represented in vernacular worship, but by the economic stratification of Catholic worshipers. The musical world is likewise fragmented and diversified, ranging in academic art composition from the quasi-total determinacy of computer-generated scores to the quasi-total indeterminacy of composers like John Cage with serialists, minimalists, resurgent romantics, and performance artists vieing for attention. The popular music world has likewise fragmented into various niches of rock, rap, jazz, musicals, country, and world music with dizzyingly changeable subcategories constantly being generated and marketed. Genuine folk music continues to be sung by some U.S. communities, but it is more frequently represented by professional folk singers who operate in an entertainment market. These multiple influences form the confusing matrix from which Roman Rite worship music will find inculturation, but a mere three decades after the Vatican Council II this musical and liturgical inculturation is still in its infancy.

Finally, the reconfiguring of Roman Catholic Church life in the aftermath of the Council continues to impact upon all its members with implications for musical leadership as well. From the exuberant late 1960s and 1970s when many worshiping communities developed local liturgical planning teams and hired professional musicians and liturgists, we seem to be entering a time of retrenchment in which the energy for local preparation of worship and the monetary resources for hiring professional pastoral musicians is disappearing. New initiatives for the liturgical and musical formation of the assembly and its ministers are a clear need.

Nevertheless the vision of Roman Catholic worship music articulated in TLS continues to inspire many who seek the glory of God and the sanctification of the faithful in sounds and silences hallowed by tradition and open to the future. The words of Pope Paul VI from an address given on 6 April 1970 to the Tenth International Congress of Church Choirs form a fitting conclusion to this study. May they inspire and encourage all who generate, participate in, lead, sustain, and evaluate the worship music of the Roman Rite in its journey "from sacred song to ritual music":

> The study of such documents clearly establishes that the charge the Church entrusts to music, its composers and performers, remains, as it has always been, one of great importance and highest purpose. Music is meant to give expression to forms of beauty that during the celebration of the liturgy will accompany the unfolding of the sacred rites and adorn the various types of the Church's prayer with the vibrant harmonies of song. Music makes the splendor of God's own countenance shine on the assembly gathered in Christ's name. The spiritual power of art helps to raise the heart more readily to the cleansing and sanctifying encounter with the luminous reality of the sacred and thus to be best disposed to celebrate the mystery of salvation and to share deeply in its effects. . . .
>
> Carry out your mission with joy, with love, with reverence, and with dedication. The sphere for your proper function is immense. . . . Do not cut yourselves off from the requirements of the rites or forget the needs of the congregation. Do not shut yourselves up, contrary to God's will, in narcissistic complacency over your . . . virtuosity and artistic abilities. Rather, know well how to give real guidance to the assembly . . . by inspiring the people to sing, by raising the level of their taste, by arousing their desire to take part. Give to the celebrations solemnity, joy, unity. This is a priceless service you are giving to the Church. . . . You must devote all your power to that service.[1]

ENDNOTE

[1] DOL no. 518, 1319–20.